The Best Gift

A Record of the Carnegie Libraries
in Ontario

by Margaret Beckman,
Stephen Langmead, John Black

"PROVIDED THROUGH A GRANT FROM THE
MINISTRY OF CITIZENSHIP AND CULTURE."

With a Foreword by the Honourable Susan Fish,
Ontario Minister of Citizenship and Culture

Dundurn Press
Toronto and London
1984

Editor: Roger Hall
Design and Production: Ron and Ron Design Photography
Typesetting: Q Composition
Printing and Binding: Laflamme & Charrier Inc. Canada

The publication of this book was made possible by support from several sources. The authors are grateful to the GEAC Corporation of Canada, and to the Armstrong Memorial Fund, University of Guelph. The publisher wishes to acknowledge the generous assistance and ongoing support of the Canada Council and the Ontario Arts Council.

The authors and publisher are especially grateful to the Ontario Heritage Foundation and to the Libraries and Community Information Branch of the Ontario Ministry of Citizenship and Culture.

Published by
Dundurn Press Limited
P.O. Box 245, Station F
Toronto, Canada
M4Y 2L5

Canadian Cataloguing in Publication Data

Beckman, Margaret, 1925-
   The best gift : a record of the Carnegie libraries
in Ontario

Bibliography: p.
Includes index.
ISBN 0-919670-82-2

1. Libraries - Ontario - Gifts, legacies.
2. Carnegie Corporation of New York. 3. Libraries -
Ontario - History. I. Langmead, Stephen, 1933-
II. Black, John B. III. Title.

Z735.O58B43 1984   027.4713   C84-098822-2

The Best Gift

A Record of the Carnegie Libraries
in Ontario

This book is dedicated to
the memory of
Keyes DeWitt Metcalf
1889–1983

Librarian of Harvard College, Emeritus

He began his library career in the decades of the Carnegie library grant
programme; his encouragement and friendship were an inspiration to
all those interested in library buildings.

Foreword

Carnegie libraries represent a significant part of the cultural history and architectural heritage of Ontario. The province's enthusiastic response to Andrew Carnegie's generosity at the turn of the century continues today in the important place libraries hold in our community life.

In many communities the Carnegie building has been spared the wrecker's ball and continues to be an integral, and frequently endangered, aspect of the architectural landscape. These libraries are a tangible reminder of a community's early commitment to ensuring the accessibility of ideas and information, a goal which is equally important today. It is particularly appropriate that during the Bicentennial of Ontario this book reminds us of this episode in our library heritage.

The Best Gift is as much a story about people as it is about buildings. Then, as today, the construction of a library building involved many dedicated persons with the common purpose of housing a library service and enhancing the cultural life of their community.

The growth of the public library community has been nothing less than dramatic. In Andrew Carnegie's day there were 118 public and 253 association libraries operating throughout the province. Eighty years later almost 100 percent of the population has access to library service including approximately 900 permanent locations holding in excess of 24 million volumes and lending more than 62 million items annually.

As the province has grown, libraries have changed to meet the needs of our multicultural society and the challenges of new technology. I am pleased that the Government of Ontario continues to play an important part in these developments.

The gifts that Andrew Carnegie gave Ontario communities serve not only to remind us of an important part of our heritage. They also remind us that although libraries have adapted to serve the needs of a changing society, the vital role they play for people in communities across the province is unchanged.

Honourable Susan Fish
Minister

List of the Carnegie Libraries of Ontario

Amherstburg
Aylmer
Ayr
Barrie
Beaverton
Berlin (Kitchener)
Bracebridge
Brampton
Brantford
Brockville
Brussels
Campbellford
Chatham
Clinton
Collingwood
Cornwall
Dresden
Dundas
Durham
Elmira
Elora
Essex
Exeter
Fergus
Forest
Fort Frances
Fort William
   (Thunder Bay)
Galt (Cambridge)
Glencoe
Goderich
Grand Valley
Gravenhurst
Grimsby
Guelph
Hamilton
Hanover
Harriston

Hespeler
   (Cambridge)
Ingersoll
Kemptville
Kenora
Kincardine
Kingsville
Leamington
Lindsay
Listowel
Lucknow
Markdale
Merritton
Midland
Milverton
Mimico(Etobicoke)
Mitchell
Mount Forest
New Hamburg
New Liskeard
Niagara Falls
North Bay
Norwich
Norwood
Orangeville
Orillia
Oshawa
Ottawa
Ottawa West Branch
Owen Sound
Palmerston
Paris
Parkhill
Pembroke
Penetanguishene
Perth
Peterborough
Picton

Port Elgin
Port Hope
Preston (Cambridge)
Renfrew
St. Catharines
St. Marys
St. Thomas
Sarnia
Sault Ste. Marie
Seaforth
Shelburne
Simcoe
Smiths Falls
Stirling
Stouffville
Stratford
Tavistock
Teeswater
Thorold
Tillsonburg
Toronto Central
   Yorkville
   Queen & Lisgar
   Riverdale
   Wychwood
   High Park
   Beaches
Toronto Junction
Walkerton
Wallaceburg
Waterloo
Watford
Welland
Weston
Whitby
Windsor
Woodstock

"What is the best gift
which can be given to a community?
. . . a free library occupies the
first place . . ."
Andrew Carnegie, 1889.

Table of Contents

Chatham Carnegie library. *The first Ontario Carnegie library was opened in Chatham on September 14, 1903.*

Preface

Our original intention in planning a book on Carnegie libraries was to provide a record—both photographic and historical —of what appeared to us to be an important part of our provincial heritage, a heritage that seemed in danger of disappearing. We had found, in our teaching assignments at the University of Western Ontario and in our work with various Public Library Boards throughout the province, that many of the original library buildings—the "Carnegie" libraries—were in need of renovation or additions in order to allow them to meet modern library objectives. We had also discovered that, unfortunately and increasingly, the libraries were being demolished to make way for new buildings. Insufficient attention was being paid to the intrinsic value of the older structures, or to the importance of the statement that they made in the urban landscape or cultural life of their communities. Windsor and Sarnia, Chatham and Guelph were among the first of the early Carnegie libraries to disappear.

The authors had all been brought up with a background of Carnegie libraries—in Waterloo and Guelph, Ontario, in Nairobi, Kenya and in London, England, and we had an emotional attachment to them. We realized, however, that our knowledge of the library buildings was confined to a vague perception that Andrew Carnegie, whose picture graced the lobbies or main reading rooms, was in some way connected with them. We embarked, therefore, on a project to assemble information about the Carnegie libraries of Ontario, naively assuming that we would need to visit and investigate perhaps fifty buildings and communities in a fairly restricted area. We soon discovered that there originally had been 111 Carnegie libraries in Ontario, from Windsor and Amherstburg in the south to New Liskeard in the north, from Kenora and Fort Frances in the west to Cornwall and Kemptville in the east. Our project became larger than we had anticipated and we spent many weekends or holidays touring the province, copying local records and taking preliminary photographs.

Our study is based on two fundamental sources: Library Board minutes from various Ontario communities as well as correspondence and clippings which have survived in local archives; and the microfilm files of the Carnegie Library Correspondence which were kindly lent to the authors by the Carnegie Corporation of New York. These latter files consist of more than 35 microfilm reels of correspondence for each of the communities in the United States, Canada, Australia, New Zealand, South

Africa and the West Indies which received a grant for a public library building. Included also is correspondence with those communities which applied for a grant but for various reasons never completed the process.

The Ontario correspondence is spread through the 35 reels, from Amherstburg to Woodstock, merged alphabetically with some 2000 American or Commonwealth towns and cities. The material in each file ranges from the initial tentative letter of request and Carnegie secretary James Bertram's responding letter of promise, through the standardized survey questionnaire and formal resolution from a Town Council which the Carnegie Corporation required. Included also are critiques of library floor plans and defending arguments from Library Boards or architects, programmes from the official openings, and inquiries from many years later seeking clarification of the Carnegie Corporation requirements. In some files there are as few as a dozen documents while in others there are more than a hundred, and in all instances the microfilm is difficult to read: handwritten letters or yellow paper carbons do not reproduce well when filmed some fifty years later. The Carnegie Corporation destroyed the original correspondence when they transferred the library building records to microfilm in the late 1940's.[1]

It should be noted that some discrepancies exist among the dates of grant requests, promise, and receipt in various publications. For instance, the *List of Library Buildings in the United States, Canada, United Kingdom and other English-speaking countries*, produced by the Carnegie Corporation of New York in 1913, (amended to 1915) includes, in the simplified spelling employed, "references to bildings erected, bildings which may be erected and bildings which may never be erected."[2] Similarly, the Ontario Department of Education Annual *Reports* from 1906 to 1910 list Carnegie libraries as completed when some were only in the grant request stage and never were finished. In determining the correct date for the final receipt of a grant the authors have depended on a later publication, *Carnegie grants for library buildings, 1890-1943*, compiled by Durand R. Miller.[3] In all instances, dates have been verified in the Carnegie Library Correspondence for each library, and these files have been used as the authority when a discrepancy has been found. Unfortunately no record was kept by the Carnegie Corporation for the dates of final completion of the library buildings. Material from individual libraries or from early newspapers has been used where those dates are given. Excerpts from letters which appear in the text are faithful to the simplified spelling which Andrew Carnegie supported and which James Bertram followed, more or less consistently. Capitalization, punctuation, spelling mistakes or omissions in the letters have also been adopted.

Illustrations fall into four categories. Coloured photographs which are grouped in the text are by John Black unless otherwise noted. The black and white photographic illustrations which accompany and explain the text are also by Black. Archival and other photographs are identified individually. The sketches by Stephen Langmead are of two kinds: water colour representations of the libraries are accurate for scale and detail; conceptual sketches and plans have been used to augment impressions of both interior and exterior features or original floor layouts.

We received support in our initial research from both the Ontario Heritage Foundation and the British Council, and visits to the Carnegie United Kingdom Trust, Edinburgh, and to the Carnegie Corporation in New York were most useful and rewarding. An appreciation of the different structures of the British and American Carnegie foundations was gained, as well as an understanding of the source records available. We were greeted with enthusiastic assistance in every library we visited, and this study could not have progressed without the material and advice so generously offered by both librarians or board members in each community.

Several individuals deserve special recognition: Win Fletcher, whose enthusiasm for the project through its several years did not falter, and who did both microfilm copying and typing; Ruth Johnston, project researcher, who assisted with the collection and collation of the archival records; and Glenda Moase, Dorothy Collins and Terry Freiburger who assisted with the word processing. The encouragement of Professor Douglas Richardson, University College, University of Toronto, is acknowledged with gratitude, as is the sensitive contribution of Professor Roger Hall, Department of History, University of Western Ontario, who edited the manuscript. Lorne Bruce, Social Science Division, University of Guelph Library provided invaluable advice about Ontario library history.

Final impetus for this publication came through a fact of history: 1984 is Ontario's bicentennial year and is an appropriate time for reflection on the province's past. Assistance received from the Libraries and Community Information Branch and the Heritage Administration Branch of the Ontario Ministry of Citizenship and Culture is most gratefully recorded. Particular gratitude is expressed to Wil Vanderelst, Director, Libraries and Community Information Branch, for his continuing interest and support.

In presenting this record of the Carnegie libraries of Ontario we have had to make difficult choices: each library has a unique story. In addition, the planning and design of each building, or the work of the various architects, provides the basis for an architectural study. What we have chosen to do is broader: to trace the Ontario Carnegie libraries from the first tentative letter of request to Carnegie officials through to the end of the building programme, letting the Town Clerks, Librarians, or Library Board Chairmen, and most importantly James Bertram, Andrew Carnegie's secretary, tell the stories in their own words. Brief descriptions of architectural features and of building design have been included, but we have concentrated on the pursuit of the library grant and on the agreement concerning "effective accommodation," which Bertram—and presumably Carnegie—considered more important. In most instances, particularly after 1907, the completion of the building was almost an anticlimax to the receipt of the grant, and to the efforts to find floor plans or library layouts which would be acceptable to Bertram.

We realize that this focus means that we cannot cover the entire subject: this study is intended to be an overview of the mechanism and achievements of the Carnegie grant programme in Ontario rather than a comprehensive study of each library or of library service during that same period. So much rich material is available in the Ontario Carnegie Library Correspondence that we made the decision to emphasize this previously unexploited record.

We also realize that this account is incomplete. We have not been able, for example, to identify an architect for every library, nor have we been able to confirm the date on which each library formally opened. As well, it has been impossible to present the same detail about each community and its particular problems. Nevertheless, we feel that the selection of material, documents, photographs and sketches convey the essence of the Carnegie library building programme in Ontario, and will provide a stepping stone to further exploration of this fascinating aspect of Ontario's history.

Margaret Beckman
Stephen Langmead
John Black
Guelph, January, 1984.

Andrew Carnegie, 1835-1919. *A print of an Andrew Carnegie portrait was hung in a prominent position in most of the Ontario Carnegie libraries.*

Introduction

Andrew Carnegie and his library philanthropy

Andrew Carnegie, 1835-1919, the Scottish immigrant boy who went on to make a fortune in the steel industry of the United States, declared his philosophy of philanthropy or trusteeship of wealth in two essays, written in 1889. In the first, "Wealth," Carnegie advocated that although the surplus funds of wealthy men should be distributed to provide for the welfare and happiness of the common man, such distribution should be as assistance, not for the total funding of a project. This admonition was due to his strong belief that no individual or group was improved by charity—or "alms giving."[1]

In his second essay, entitled "The best fields for philanthropy" he listed what he considered to be worthy of philanthropy as universities, libraries, medical centers, public parks, meeting and concert halls, public baths and churches. But the "best gift" that could be given to a community, he suggested, was a free library, "provided the community will accept and maintain it as a public institution, as much a part of the city property as its public schools, and, indeed, as an adjunct to these."[2]

Carnegie's interest in libraries began early in his life. His father, William Carnegie, a craft weaver in Dunfermline, Scotland, had been an original member of a Tradesman's Library which had been established from a pooling of his own books and those of two fellow weavers. This was the first circulating library in that town.[3]

The family immigrated to the United States in 1848 hoping to escape the industrialization of the weaving trade, and Andrew Carnegie's formal education ended. In 1850, as a teenage telegraphic messenger boy in Allegheny, Pennsylvania, Carnegie, with other apprentices, borrowed books from the private library of Colonel James Anderson. Later, when this collection was expanded to become the "Mechanics and Apprentices Library" with a $2.00 annual subscription fee for all but apprentices, Carnegie wrote a successful letter to the Pittsburgh *Dispatch* under the pseudonym of 'A Working Boy,' arguing that any fee should be eliminated.[4] He never forgot this early association with Allegheny's first free public library, nor the importance of Anderson's benefaction to his education and life.

When Andrew Carnegie retired in 1901 and sold the Carnegie Steel Company to J.P. Morgan, he received $500,000,000. Placed in various trusts this money was the basis for the philanthropy which then became his full-time occupation, although he had already begun his "giving" with a public swimming bath (1877) and then a public library (1883) in his hometown of Dunfermline.[5] By 1895, five years after his essay on "Wealth" appeared, he had also endowed library buildings, and in some instances the collections as well, in Edinburgh, Aberdeen, Ayr, Wick, Stirling, Jedburg, Peterhead and Inverness, Scotland and in Allegheny, Braddock and Pittsburgh, Pennsylvania and Fairfield, Iowa.[6]

In total, Andrew Carnegie, or the Carnegie Corporation which succeeded his personal giving in 1911, donated a total of $56,162,622.97 to free public library buildings world-wide, with $2,556,660 granted for library construction in Canada.[7] Table 1 illustrates the location of those buildings throughout the English speaking world.

Table 1   Free public library buildings[8]

Location	Number of buildings	Amount $
United States	1,681	41,233,853.47
Canada	125	2,556,660.00
Australia	4	68,240.00
New Zealand	18	207,397.00
South Africa	12	123,855.00
West Indies	6	97,355.00
Various	3	25,805.00
Great Britain and Ireland	660	11,849,457.50
Total	2,509	56,162,622.97

It should be realized that although public libraries remained the primary focus of Andrew Carnegie's philanthropy they were not his sole interest. Scientific research, advancement of teaching, the furthering of international peace, the reward of heroic deeds and the provision of church organs were among the better known of his public benefactions. Academic library buildings, primarily in the United States but including Victoria College, University of Toronto, were also funded, and library collections, special libraries (such as at dental schools), library education, library associations and library demonstration projects were all well supported. Such library interests in Canada had received $611,400 prior to 1935 from the Carnegie Corporation of New York.[9]

Of the 125 Carnegie libraries completed in Canada the greatest number, 111, were in Ontario, as Table 2 indicates. Two factors at least partially explain this preponderance: one was the history of library development in this province. The other was the relatively early urban settlement of Ontario and the popular recognition of the need for free or public libraries. The pattern of obtaining a Carnegie library building was similar, however, whether in the American states or in the provinces of Canada, and the influence of Andrew Carnegie upon library services in Ontario, and to a lesser degree on the rest of Canada, has a visible reminder in the many Carnegie libraries which continue to serve their original purpose.

Table 2   Carnegie libraries in Canada[10]

Location	Number of buildings	Amount $
Alberta	3	217,500
British Columbia	3	121,915
Manitoba	4	201,000
New Brunswick	1	50,000
Ontario	111	1,866,745
Saskatchewan	2	14,500
Yukon	1	25,000
Total	125	2,556,660

London Public Library, 1895, enlarged 1903. *London already had a library building when the Carnegie grant programme began in Ontario, and was one of the few larger communities which did not apply for a grant.*

Chapter One

Ontario libraries
before 1900

The Scottish background of many of the early Ontario settlers had a direct influence on the development of libraries in this province, since parochial, presbyterial, and synodical lending libraries were familiar institutions in Scotland from the beginning of the eighteenth century. Although there are some references to private collections and group readings in Ontario prior to 1800, the first library for which records exist was that of Newark (Niagara-on-the-Lake) established June 8 of that year. It was a subscription library with an annual fee of $4.00.[1]

Other subscription libraries followed, for example in Kingston, although fees of even $1.00 per year were considered too much for many households, and free libraries became a popular project for philanthropists. A Quaker library, open to all, was established in Machell's Corners (later Aurora) in the early 1820's, and in 1830 merchant James Lesslie established a free lending library for his employees in the Town of York (now Toronto). Attempts to establish subscription libraries in what was to become Toronto did not prosper: library services in York began in 1810 but were abandoned after the American raid during the War of 1812, and Egerton Ryerson's attempt to start a York subscription library in 1827 failed.[2]

The early subscription libraries were replaced by Mechanics' Institutes beginning in the 1830's, with the first two established at Kingston and Toronto. These institutions co-existed through the 1830's and 1840's with somewhat different forms to their activities. The subscription libraries existed solely to lend books, while the Mechanics' Institutes were intended to provide their members—"mechanics and workingmen"— with lectures, classes, reading rooms and lending libraries. In addition to the earliest two, this period saw the development of Mechanics' Institutes in Brantford, Dundas, Hamilton, London, Paris and Niagara. Toronto had a Mechanics' Institute and two subscriptions libraries as well as Lesslie's library before 1850.[3]

In 1835 the government of Upper Canada officially recognized the importance of libraries with special Acts for the Mechanics' Institutes of Toronto and Kingston providing grants of $800 and $400 (200 and 100 pounds sterling) respectively, although such money was for scientific equipment as much as for books.[4] Library development in the next three decades was slowed, however, due to a confusion in the roles of the subscription libraries and Mechanics' Institutes. An 1851 Act of the Legislative Assembly of Canada provided for the incorporation and better management of Library Associations and Mechanics' Institutes, [5] but grants were to be provided to the Mechanics' Institutes only and even these ceased in 1858. The government evidently preferred that the Institutes emphasize the direct role of education by providing lectures or evening classes.[6] In 1857 the Legislature established The Board of Arts and Manufactures for Upper Canada, whose duty was to develop a system of elementary, practical, and vocational education for mechanics, artisans and manufactures and in addition to supply the sons of farmers and others with opportunities for obtaining practical knowledge of agriculture, chemistry and mechanics. Incorporated Mechanics' Institutes were entitled to memberships on the Board and to participate in the management. However, funding was never sufficient for such an ambitious programme, especially in a time of recession.[7]

Common School Libraries, housed in school buildings and operated by the local boards of school trustees, were open to students, teachers and local residents and were the predecessors of the first public library system in Ontario. Egerton Ryerson, Chief Superintendent of Education for Upper Canada, 1844-1876, was directly responsible for this development, having been impressed by the establishment of district school libraries in the United States.[8] The Act for the Better Establishment and Maintenance of Common Schools in Upper Canada, [9] empowered school trustees for cities, towns, villages or rural sections to establish Common School Libraries, with the larger jurisdictions enabled to establish travelling libraries as well. This 1850 Act and later amendments provided the financial support for libraries by a general tax rate upon property as well as through provincial grants equal to the amounts contributed locally. The school libraries were unfortunately restricted in their collection building to the 4,000 titles listed in a general catalogue supplied by the Department of Public Instruction, and after the recession of 1857 school trustees commonly purchased fewer volumes from the Depository of the Upper Canada Educational Department. The public once more would require the local Mechanics' Institute libraries for their additional reading material.[10]

In an effort to support the library function of the Mechanics' Institutes, the Board of Arts and Manufactures established a Provincial Reference Library of technical books for the use of the Institutes, financed initially by the Bureau of Agriculture. The Minister of Agriculture and the Board of Arts and Manufactures also initiated a classified catalogue of books appropriate for agriculture, architecture, science, fine arts, travel and history in addition to technical trades but the Institute libraries were not restricted to this list in their book purchases.[11]

The expansion of the Institute libraries and the decline of those in the school system led the Legislature to transfer, once again, responsibility for public library service from the schools to the Institutes in 1873, at the same time amending the Agriculture and Arts Act to allow provincial grants to be used for books of philosophy, poetry and biography as well as in those subjects listed above.

In 1880, Adam Crooks, first Ontario Minister of Education, transferred responsibility for the Institutes from the Department of Agriculture to the Department of Education. His intention was to establish free libraries in cities, towns and villages, to permit the Institutes' libraries to continue in unincorporated communities or rural areas, and to disband the Book Depository for public school libraries. A survey of the Mechanics' Institutes undertaken by Dr. Samual Passmore May, Superintendent of the Educational Library and Museums, contained a strong indictment of the Institutes. May's survey, which was issued in 1881 as "Special Report of the Minister of Education on the Mechanics' Institutes" (Ontario), did not specifically address the problems of free public libraries.[12] However, while the Agriculture and Arts Act allowed the Institutes to continue, the year 1882 saw the passage of the Free Libraries Act.[13] This Act permitted municipalities to levy a maximum of one-half mill as a "Free Library Rate," after local rate payers had approved the establishment of a Free Library in a plebiscite. Both the Institute libraries, which remained reliant on a $400 legislative grant, and the Free Libraries with their local tax levy, co-existed for the next several years.

In 1895 the government attempted to resolve this problem of library duplication with consolidation of all previous legislation in an Act to Amend and Consolidate the Acts respecting Free Libraries and Mechanics' Institutes, which allowed free public libraries and public libraries, not free.[14] The Act also encouraged the libraries to take over some of the educational functions of the Institutes, leading to the importance of the lecture room as an element of the library building. Government support for the libraries continued to be less than adequate by today's standards, with annual book grants limited to $200 for cities, $150 for towns, and $100 for all other jurisdictions. An additional $50 was provided for newspapers and magazines in existing reading rooms, and $100 for evening classes.[15] The demand for public library services did not diminish and by 1900 there were 118 free public and 253 public (not free) libraries operating in Ontario.[16] The Ontario Library Association, created in 1900, was a clear response to this invigorated library interest, and increasingly assumed the role of agitating for improved library support and legislation.

Physical facilities for the expanding libraries was another matter, and it was not uncommon for one set of inadequate rented rooms to be exchanged for another every few years. Few Ontario communities—Toronto, Hamilton and London being the most notable exceptions—had separate library buildings before the turn of the century.

News of the availability of grants for library buildings reached Ontario as early as 1899, and was greeted by most of those who heard or read about Andrew Carnegie's library philanthropy with enthusiasm. The impact of the provision of new and permanent physical facilities for the 371 Ontario communities with libraries, as well as for those as yet without was, not unexpectedly, dramatic. Actually securing the grants, however, would prove a considerable challenge to all.

James Bertram, 1872-1934. *Bertram was secretary to Andrew Carnegie from 1897 to 1914, and served as secretary of the Carnegie Corporation of New York from 1911 to 1934. He personally approved, on behalf of Carnegie, all the Ontario library grants, and after 1907 he insisted on approving the library building plans, as well.*

Chapter Two

"Letter of promise" 1899-1917

The building grants programme

Besides Andrew Carnegie himself, who after the first few years was fairly remote from day to day procedures, the library building grants programme was managed by two individuals: James Bertram, Carnegie's private secretary, and Robert A. Franks, his financial agent. Bertram was a fellow Scot who had been hired by Carnegie in 1897, after a period of work in railways and mining in South Africa. Recommended to Carnegie by a former teacher, James Matthew, and by Hew Morrison, chief librarian of the Edinburgh Public Library, Bertram was twenty-five years old when he first joined Carnegie and began his involvement with the library philanthropy.[1]

Faced with thousands of applications for a share of Carnegie's fortune Bertram quickly found it necessary to "bring order out of chaos, to organize the office, to devise ways and means by which the requests should be handled in a competent, orderly, and effective manner."[2] He established procedures to cover every contingency and, within a framework of questionnaires and resolutions, he attempted to ensure that "each worthy request received careful and serious consideration." Bertram was helpful to those making application but he believed strongly that "contracts, once entered into, should be lived up to in all particulars" and "that the prodigal distribution of money would cause more harm than good."[3]

Since it was Bertram who, in the final analysis, determined if a library building grant was to be awarded, the grant recipients soon found it necessary to understand and cope with his idiosyncracies. They discovered that he was "methodical and systematic in all things, a stickler for precedent. He never used a paragraph when a sentence would do; and a word often served to take the place of a sentence."[4] Moreover, like Carnegie, Bertram used a simplified spelling (e.g. wel for well, hav for have) that must have caused considerable confusion for the Library Boards and Town Councils receiving his letters.

Interestingly, Carnegie's support of simplified spelling provides another link to libraries, for the co-founder of the movement was Melvil Dewey, who also developed the Dewey Decimal system for the classification of books. Dewey's argument that the simplification of English spelling would be a major step in making the English language the common language of the whole world appealed to Carnegie. With world peace one of his most ardent causes, he saw the possibility of having all men able to communicate with each other in the same language as an effective agency in meeting his goal. He supported the National Simplified Spelling Board from 1903 until 1915, withdrawing his annual contribution at that time due to disappointment in the results. Although President Theodore Roosevelt was an early convert to the idea, and signed a pledge card promising to use simplified spelling for twelve words—program, catalog, decatalog, prolog, demagog, tho, altho, thoro, thorofare, thru and thruout—there was insufficient support from the literary and journalistic community to make the idea popular.[5] Bertram, however, used simplified spelling until Carnegie's death in 1919.

Bertram served as Carnegie's secretary from 1897 to 1914, and was secretary to the Carnegie Corporation of New York from 1911-1934.[6] During that time he personally approved, on behalf of Carnegie, each library building grant, and eventually the building plans as well. Bertram himself received advice on libraries from W.H. Brett, librarian for the Cleveland Public Library, and frequently sent plans either to him or to Edwin H. Anderson, Chief Librarian, Carnegie Library of Pittsburgh, for criticism or advice as to changes. It was Brett who assisted in the preparation of "Notes on the Erection of Library Bildings" a pamphlet which was distributed to all libraries requesting grants after 1911.[7] In Ontario, Bertram additionally sought assistance from the government's Inspectors of Public Libraries, requesting them to investigate situations which his brisk letters seemed unable to resolve.

When Bertram had satisfied himself that a grant application and then the building plans were in order, authorization would be given to Robert A. Franks, Carnegie's financial agent, to release money from the Carnegie Foundation for the library construction. Not infrequently, when Carnegie and Bertram were in Scotland where they resided for six months of each year, Franks also assumed some of Bertram's approval duties. For the most part, however, Ontario Library Boards and Town Councils knew Franks only as the man in New Jersey who wrote the cheques, once Bertram had given approval. As might be expected, Franks released the funds in measured amounts, matching the construction schedules of the libraries. In the case of a few Ontario communities such as Hanover he became involved, unwillingly, in conflicts between Bertram and the Town Council or Library Board.[8]

Bertram and Franks were, with Carnegie, the Executive Committee of the Board of Trustees for the Carnegie Corporation of New York, formed, as noted, in 1911. Until 1917 and the cessation of the building grants, all action was taken by the Committee, with formal approval given by the Board at the annual meeting. "Because of their unusually capable and untiring service and loyal devotion," Bertram and Franks were named life trustees of the Corporation and awarded $5000 annuities, in addition to their salaries.[9]

James Bertram, incidentally, has a link to Ontario in addition to the major role which he played in the Carnegie library grants. In 1904 he married Janet Tod Ewing of Seaforth, and when he died in 1934 at the age of 62 his body was transported by train to Seaforth, where he is buried in the Maitlandbank cemetery.[10]

ANDREW CARNEGIE,
2 EAST 91ST STREET,
NEW YORK.

Please address further communi-
cations to Mr. R. A. Franks, Home
Trust Company, Hoboken, N. J., who
will now have charge of the correspondence regarding your ~~Organ~~. *Library.*

Carnegie Corporation form re payment. *This is one of the forms developed after Bertram assumed control of the grant programmes. Note that the same form was used for organs, and Library was simply written in.*

ANDREW CARNEGIE
2 EAST 91ST ST.

New York; April 26, 1907.

H. V. Knight, Esq.,
    Sec'y., Library Board,
        Woodstock, Ont.

Dear Sir,

Yours of 22nd April received, also the plans,
which have been returned. Your adoption of the rotunda
feature raised the expenditures on the building considerably,
and ~~is~~ also *Causes m to be* somewhat lavish in space in the way of hall,
etc. Please send a statement showing the assessed valuation
of Woodstock for the year 1900 and each succeeding year,
showing also the basis of assessment.

Respectfully yours,

Jas Bertram

P. Secretary.

A Bertram letter. *Note that this letter, like the form, has handwritten corrections, and is one of the few examples of Bertram's use of correct, rather than simplified spelling.*

27

Table 3   Ontario Library Grants approved in 1901[1]

Windsor .... February 13
Collingwood .... August 16
Guelph .... October 17
Ottawa (Main) .... November 6
Sault Ste. Marie .... December 14
Stratford .... December 14
Cornwall .... December 21
St. Catharines .... December 31

Collingwood Carnegie library. *The first recorded request for an Ontario library building grant came from Collingwood on June 8, 1899. Typically, it made reference to the Scottish background of the community, and heaped praise on the potential benefactor, Andrew Carnegie.*

1901: the first Ontario grants

In the early days of Carnegie library grants only two conditions had to be met, and these had to be stated in a formal letter from town officials: first, the community should provide the site; and second, the City or Town Council should appropriate by taxation not less than 10 per cent of the cost of the building for annual maintenance (i.e. books and staff). As simple as this procedure may sound it frequently took many letters and more months or even years before the requirements were met to Bertram's satisfaction. Neither was it unusual for letters to go unanswered for quite some time owing to Carnegie and Bertram's frequent moves between New York and Scotland. The confusion caused by these delays or by letters crossing in the mail often led to a caustic exchange.

It is difficult to verify which was the first community in Ontario to act upon the possibility of a grant. The Carnegie Corporation of New York acknowledges eight applications for library building grants approved in 1901, as shown in the following table.

Although Windsor received the first approval for a Carnegie library grant, the Carnegie Library Correspondence reveals that the first letter from an Ontario community requesting consideration was written not from Windsor but from Collingwood on June 8, 1899, and addressed to Andrew Carnegie, on United States Consulate paper:

Honored and dear Sir:

I have the honor to enclose herewith an authenticated statement of the condition of the public library of this town, together with a personal letter addressed to you by its President, Mr. Henry Robertson, Q.C. and a fellow Scot. The representations contained therein, I need scarcely say, may be implicitedly [sic] relied upon.

Since I took up my residence here, about 18 months ago, as Consul of the United States for this section of the country, embracing all the places situate on Georgian Bay, and including the Consular Agencies at Owen Sound, Parry Sound, Barrie and Lindsay, no matter of local interest has interested me more than the library question, the intellectual development, as well as the happiness and prosperity of the entire community being so nearly dependent thereon, and I should be greatly gratified if you should find it convenient to respond to Mr. Robertson's appeal in its behalf. The case, I assure you, is a most urgent and deserving one.

Permit me also to avail myself of this occassion [sic] to express to you my heart felt thanks and gratitude for the munificient [sic] gift, $250,000, which you recently made, through my esteemed friend and classmate, Mr. B.H. Warner, for a public library at my home city, Washington, D.C.

A native of Scotland myself, and for many years Secretary of St. Andrew's Society, Washington, D.C., I feel safe in saying that every Scotchman there, as well as throughout the world are proud of the name and fame of Andrew Carnegie, and share with me the earnest hope and trust that he will be long blessed with life, health, happiness and prosperity; also that he may realise in fullest measure the satisfaction which comes from good works, and a well spent life, and in the reflection, that, from purely philanthropic and humanitarian motives, he has contributed so largely and successfully towards improving the moral, intellectual and physical condition of the human family, whenever and wherever it has been in his power so to do. Surely the world has never known a greater public benefactor.[2]

This letter was signed by William Small, and enclosed with it was a statement from the President of the Collingwood Public Library Board, Henry Robertson, officially requesting money for a library building. Whether or not the idea for seeking Carnegie's assistance came from Small's association with Washington is interesting to speculate. Whatever the reason for the initial letter, it was almost two years before the Collingwood Council's guarantee of support would satisfy Bertram's strict requirements.

That first year of the Ontario Carnegie library grants—1901—was typical of those which followed, as Library Boards and Town or City Councils struggled to determine how best to justify their request for the money, what they could include in the building, and how they could plan the exterior. Almost without exception they found that they could not manage on the initial grant, and repeated requests for additional funds to "finish the library in a fitting manner" were made. Some were successful, some not. Bertram's reticence, as displayed in his correspondence, often hindered rather than helped the process, and only the persistence of Library Boards, Mayors or Town Clerks kept many projects alive to completion. The first eight Ontario communities to receive the promise of a Carnegie grant established patterns for the province which would continue through the next two decades. Their experience is chronicled below.

Windsor

Although Collingwood had made the first request in 1899, Windsor received the first formal "letter of promise" on February 13, 1901. Five letters had been sent to Andrew Carnegie in Pittsburgh, New York, and at Skibo Castle, Scotland, from January 25 through November 19, 1900, before a response was received. The fifth letter, January 25, 1901, written by Board Secretary Andrew Braid on St. Andrew's Society letterhead appealed "to a Scot from a Scottish society," and evinced the following, very typical, Bertram response:

> Windsor should hav a Free Public Library, having 11,000 people, and if the town wil furnish a proper site and agree to tax itself to maintain a library to the extent of $1,500 a year, which is about the minimum for which a library can be operated, I shal be glad to giv, say, $20,000 for a suitable bilding. Mr. Carnegie is not disposed to giv money for libraries unless he is sure of their being maintained by the community."[3]

Difficulties arose before approval to accept this kind offer was received from Windsor City Council, due to vigorous opposition by some Council members to the cost of the building site which the Library Board had selected. Braid's letter to Bertram in May, 1901, suggested that there might be some problems but he only hinted at the cause of the delay.

> I think it advisable to write you that although Mr. Carnegie's offer regarding a library building for Windsor has not yet been accepted by the city council, there is not the slightest doubt about its being taken advantage of, as all the councillors are favorably disposed. The reason for its non-acceptance is that the different parties who are now quietly getting options on suitable properties for a site may thus perhaps be able to get reasonable figures, whereas if the offer was definitely closed with the owners of the properties might raise their prices. The city council have a committee dealing with the matter in conjunction with the members of the library board of management.[4]

Windsor Carnegie library. *Windsor received the first official promise of a Carnegie grant in Ontario, in what Bertram called the "letter of promis," on February 13, 1901. Difficulties in securing approval of a site for the new library delayed construction so that Windsor was not the first Ontario Carnegie library to be completed.*

Table 4   First 10 Carnegie library openings[7]

Library	Date of grant	Date of opening
Chatham	February 13, 1902	September 14, 1903
Stratford	December 14, 1901	September 19, 1903
Windsor	February 13, 1901	October 16, 1903
Sarnia	January 10, 1902	November 26, 1903
Berlin	March 14, 1902	January 9, 1904
Smiths Falls	January 23, 1902	February 25, 1904
Lindsay	January 23, 1902	June 28, 1904
Brantford	April 11, 1902	July 1, 1904
Paris	January 2, 1903	July 27, 1904
Brockville	April 13, 1903	August 13, 1904

A clipping from *The Evening Record*, included with the Minutes of the Windsor Board Meeting for February, 1902, records the final approval by City Council for the site purchase, after almost eight months of wrangling over both site costs and locations.

> That some of the aldermen of the City Council are not lacking in finesse and native shrewdness was evidenced last night when there was a labored discussion to kill time until an absent member arrived to record his vote. A strenuous fight was in progress over the question of voting additional money for the library site, and when it was manifest that the vote would be close, a telephone message was sent to Ald. N.A. Bartlet, who was ill in bed, that his presence was absolutely required. He reached the hall just in time to turn apparent defeat into glorious victory."[5]

Further delays to the building occurred when contractors' bids were higher than the amount of money promised, and only Braid's persistence in securing two additional grants (bringing the total to $27,000) allowed the building to be completed.

Years later Braid wrote to Bertram, asking for confirmation that Windsor was the first city in Canada to receive a gift from Mr. Carnegie. Bertram's answer, dated February 23, 1917, was a compromise:

> So far as my chronological register goes, the first promis to a city in Canada by Mr. Carnegie for the erection of a library bilding was that made to Windsor. I am not so sure about its being the first bilding erected, however. The records show that the last payments on four other library bildings wer before the last payment was made on the Windsor bilding. It may hav been that the Windsor bilding was substantially completed before those others."[6]

The delays in securing Council approval for the site purchase had resulted in Windsor moving from first to third in terms of the official opening, as illustrated in Table 4, although only a few days or weeks separated the first three completed Ontario Carnegie library buildings.

Collingwood

Collingwood was quite ambitious, proposing in their initial application that the town planned to use the requested $25,000 for more than a library. The Council hoped to solve what would appear to be an early instance of juvenile delinquency:

> Besides the Library proper and the book-stacks and Reading rooms, there should be a Gymnasium for Young Men and one for Women, a Swimming Bath, a Camera room, a Lecture room, a Childrens' room, a Recreation room, etc., and the Board believe that with the sum of $25,000 they could erect a suitable Building having all these features.
>
> With such a building, the very troublesome problem of what we are to do with our boys in the evenings would be solved in this neighborhood, and they would have cause to bless the liberality that enabled them to have such advantages.
>
> With much respect and admiration for your unparalleled generosity, We beg to remain, ...[8]

Bertram's brief promise two weeks later of a grant for $12,500 made no mention of the elaborate request. However, in June, 1904 the Collingwood Library Board wrote again to Carnegie, explaining that while the building was completed, "an ornament of the town and a credit to all concerned," it had cost $14,000 and the Library was in debt. After requesting copies of the plans, census figures for Collingwood's population (then 6,000), a detailed list of all expenditures, and a guarantee that the Town Council would increase its grant appropriately, an additional $2,000 was received and the building completed.[9]

Guelph

Guelph also had to request an additional grant when their original plans, prepared by Guelph architect W. Frye Colwill, were tendered at $25,000, $5,000 more than their grant. Financial agent R.A. Franks became involved at this time, and he was not disposed to increase the grant until he had received a judgement on the proposed plans from someone he thought competent—Edwin H. Anderson, Chief Librarian of the Pittsburgh Carnegie Public Library. Their exchange, in October and November, 1902, contains comments which are among the most severely critical of any Ontario library in the Carnegie Correspondence files.

> Will you kindly oblige me by giving me your opinion of the enclosed sketch of the proposed Library Building at Guelph, Ont. I am inclined to believe it is not a very good building for $25,000.00, the amount they say it will cost, which is $5,000 above their appropriation.
> I cannot very well put the question of increase before Mr. Carnegie with the sketch of the building they have sent as I think it could be very much improved upon.
> The Auditorium and platform are entirely too large, if needed at all, and I do not see any need of the large dressing rooms on either side of the platform. A lecture room half the size of the Auditorium I would consider large enough and the rest of the space could be used as a children's room. On the ground floor plan I do not think the stack room is large enough, while I do not see the need of the Board room and Secretary's room on this floor. The Magazine room is large compared with the other rooms.[10]

Anderson's response was equally strong:

> I am bound to say that these plans do not impress me favorably. I had some correspondence last spring with the Secretary of their Board, Mr. James E. Day, and sent them some suggestions for library plans in accordance with their request. They seem to have deliberately chosen a grandiloquent and expensive exterior, and allowed the interior to take care of itself. The exterior seems to be what has been called the 'pillarsham' style. The floor plan is so inadequate that it seems hardly worth while to criticise it in detail. There is no children's room, nor librarian's office, nor catalogue room. There are rooms however for the Board of Trustees and its secretary, neither of which is needed. The necessary rooms should be provided first, and if there is any room or money left for a small lecture room, all well and good.
> It is difficult to get a good floor plan with a corner entrance. It

may be very beautiful on the outside, but there is no need for it on the kind of lot they seem to have. I would suggest that you disapprove these plans as well as their request for an addition $5,000. They have not shown any special qualifications for spending money.[11]

The Guelph Library Board reluctantly made changes to the plans, reducing the outside ornamentation and assigning the proposed Secretary and Board Rooms to the Librarian and to cataloguing, but still felt they would need additional funds. Bertram was not happy, as his December, 1902 letter to Franks indicates, and he gave initial approval for only the $20,000:

> Please act on the authority which you have regarding Guelph, Ont. Although the building is not the best that might be chosen for the circumstances of Guelph, I do not think Mr. Carnegie would like to go further than point this out as has already been done.[12]

After two more years of pleas from the Guelph Library Board, and with assurance of increased support from the Town Council, the grant was finally increased to $24,000.

Ottawa

The capital city of Ottawa, which requested a grant of "about $60,000 to build a library similar to Hamilton's" was surprised to receive approval for $100,000 in March, 1901. Disturbed that there would be unused space in the resulting library, Mayor Fred W. Cook wrote in July, 1902:

> My particular object in writing you at this juncture is to ask whether there would be any objection on your part to us using a portion of the basement of the proposed building as a public swimming bath, of which this City is very much in need. There will be considerable available space in the basement, but we would not like to make such a change without the consent of the donor of the building.[13]

With firm admonitions from Bertram that the grant was to be used only for a library building, and after delays caused by disagreement over a site and the bankruptcy of a contractor, the Ottawa library was finally completed in 1906. At that time a rare distinction was accorded the City in that Andrew Carnegie himself, who was visiting Canada and making speeches "of a cheery and optimistic but thoroughly Americanized view of things British and Canadian," opened the new Carnegie Library.[14] Ottawa was the only one of the Ontario libraries which Carnegie opened, although he paid a brief visit to the Smiths Falls Library on the same occasion.

In spite of Mayor Cook's concern that a building costing $100,000 would be too large, by 1913—only seven years after completion—the Ottawa librarian wrote to Carnegie asking for a $25,000 grant with which to extend the Library. He noted that the "Reading Room and Reference Room were often filled in the late afternoon and evening, and people have to turn away." Bertram's response expressed perfectly the later policy of the Carnegie Corporation toward grants for the larger cities:

Guelph Carnegie library. *The building was severely criticized by the Chief Librarian of the Pittsburgh Carnegie Public Library, Edwin H. Anderson, who was asked to review the plans before an additional grant was considered. He called the building "grandiloquent and expensive, of the pillar-sham" style.*

Sault Ste. Marie Carnegie library. *The first Carnegie library in Sault Ste. Marie, completed in 1904, was destroyed by fire in 1907. Because it was next door to the Fire Station, the Town Council had neglected to insure it for its full value and it took considerable persuasion before Bertram agreed to sufficient funds to complete a 'second' Carnegie library for Sault Ste. Marie. The Library is the middle building of the three building complex in the above photograph.*

We do not consider the claims of large cities for central library bildings especially when they hav alredy been supplied with a bilding. In cities of the size and importance of Ottawa only the provision of branch library bildings where necessary is included in the scope of work of Carnegie Corporation of New York.[15]

Ottawa eventually acted on this advice, and received a grant for their West Branch in 1916.

Sault Ste. Marie

An interesting situation in Sault Ste. Marie led to their request for a further grant. The original grant of $10,000 allowed them to complete their Library, although without new furnishings, by the spring of 1904. However, on March 18, 1907, the Town Clerk of Sault Ste. Marie, C.J. Pim, wrote to Robert Franks that: "You will be sorry to hear that the Carnegie Library was destroyed by fire on the 7th, last, together with our Municipal buildings and Fire Hall . . . ."[16]

In a subsequent letter a grant of $5,500 was requested, which, with $4,500 received from the insurance, would be sufficient to rebuild the library. Bertram was extremely annoyed, writing that ". . . in the first place, your building should have been insured for Ten Thousand Dollars," and asking for some explanation. In November, 1907, Town Clerk Pim finally admitted that "the only reason that can be given is that the Town Fire Hall and the Library were so close together that both were considered as absolutely safe from destruction by fire."[17] This last resulted in the following caustic comment from Bertram: "The fact that the building was insured for $4500 does not bear out your statement that it was considered absolutely safe from destruction by fire. Sault Ste. Marie seems to have been penny wise in this matter."[18]

Bertram wrote again, in April 1908, requesting further assurance that the "Library Building would be ensured to its full cost and value" before he finally agreed to the second grant of $5,500.[19]

Stratford

The Stratford Carnegie Library, which is the only one still in use from the first year of the Ontario grants, had more difficulty than most communities in securing a grant because of opposition from the public:

> From different quarters came protests against accepting donations from Carnegie whose wealth was deemed 'blood money' by many folk, especially by those affiliated with labor unions. At a labor mass meeting one of the speakers declared that Carnegie came to his wealth by crooked schemes. Acceptance of the millionaire's donation was strongly denounced and it was alleged that Council should not erect monuments to self glorification.[20]

However, a determined Board and Council proceeded quietly to accept the grant—even to have it increased from $12,000 to $15,000—and the Library opened without fanfare in September, 1903. Within three years the Board claimed that more space was needed and Board member Russell Stuart wrote Bertram in April, 1906, asking for additional funds, explaining the problem that they had had with the initial grant.

Stratford Carnegie library. *Stratford is the only Carnegie library which remains from the first year of the Carnegie library grants in Ontario. Strong opposition from local labour unions to accepting Carnegie money almost prevented Stratford from receiving a library building grant.*

Cornwall Carnegie library. *A corner turret with a conical roof was part of this building when it was opened in 1904. This ornamentation was removed before the above photograph was taken, although the line of the turret can be identified. Even without the turret the Cornwall design was unique in the province, although it is believed to have had an infuence on the plans for the Bracebridge Carnegie library.*

The Board would gladly have qualified under the terms of your offer for a grant of $18,000 but for the illiberal attitude of the Municipal Council largely controlled at that time by a fanatical labor element made this impossible.[21]

When this request was turned down nothing more was done until 1910, when another Library Board member, J. Davis Barnett, wrote to ask for funds for an extension. When he received floor plans for the proposed addition in 1911, Bertram expressed his feelings to Barnett with a touch of sarcasm:

> On referring back to the correspondence, we find that you were the party who originally was the recipient on behalf of the city of Mr. Carnegie's gift of $12,000 for a Library Bilding. When he agreed to increase the amount to $15,000 he had a rite to expect that care would be taken that a Library Bilding complete and redy to occupy would be secured. There seems to hav been mismanagement, however, from the start, inasmuch as in your letter of December 8, 1910, you propose to spend another gift from Mr. Carnegie partly to finish the inside rough walls and furnishing the top floor auditorium, etc.
>
> You propose in your program providing a public bath and fittings and apparently the provision of living accommodation. Mr. Carnegie provided money for a public library bilding, not a public bath bilding or a dwelling . . . A janitor normally has one room, if he has any. In the additional part there are three rooms added, markt Janitor, nine in all. Surely some explanation is needed here . . .
>
> In the revised plan you show a stack room about three times the size of the reading room, which is absurd. In a stack room 76 feet by 52 could be shelved many many thousands more of books than Stratford could hope to purchase in many years . . . .[22]

Barnett attempted to justify the proposed plans, explaining that the large stack room was needed because it was open to the public and continued:

> As to the janitor's place—he has always lived in the basement, and when you remember the ordinary rigour of our climate, and the fact that we are on the topside of the water-shed between the great lakes, more than 900 ft. above Lake Ontario, there is justification for the caretaker's living on the premises . . . The suggested addition to the basement under the new stack rooms was made so that every room used would have natural light and ventilation, leaving the old blindrooms vacant. The difference in cost between leaving the basement as an earth floored cellar, or utilizing it for sanitary living is $528.[23]

His explanation did not dissuade Bertram from his views, and no further Carnegie funds were received in Stratford.

Cornwall

The town of Cornwall received its promise of $7,000 for a library building in December, 1901 after filling in the "Schedule of Questions," shown below, which Bertram sent to all libraries when he received an initial request:

Free Public Library

Town: *Cornwall, Ontario*

Population: *Seven thousand (7,000.)*

Has it a Library at present: *Yes*

Amount Taxes Paid by Community Yearly for Support:
  Five hundred dollars ($500.00)

Amount Guaranteed from Taxes Yearly if Building
  Obtained: *Seven hundred dollars ($700.00)*

Is Requisite Site Available: *Yes*

Amount now Collected toward Building: *Nothing yet as
  it has always been housed in leased premises*

To facilitate Mr. Carnegie's consideration of your
  appeal, will you oblige by filling in the above?

Respectfully,

Jas. Bertram

Secretary[24]

It was not until June of the following year that Cornwall began to plan for its Library, and John Chisholm, a member of the Building Committee, wrote to Carnegie asking if he could "give us the address of some architects who have published books of designs for public buildings, including public libraries, so that we may have something before us from which to make a satisfactory selection."[25] This request was referred to Anderson, the Pittsburgh librarian, but unfortunately there is no record of any recommendation. The Cornwall Library was completed with an additional grant of $1,000 in 1904.

St. Catharines

St. Catharines was also typical of the communities that could not complete their library within the limits of the initial grant. The $20,000 promised in December, 1901 was increased by $5,000 in 1903, when the architect could not adjust his plans sufficiently to bring the construction tenders under $20,000. St. Catharines Mayor J.B. McIntyre had written a persuasive letter, explaining the situation in considerable detail:

> When our City Council accepted your very liberal offer of twenty thousand dollars they decided to have the library erected on the City Hall plot—we called for plans and received sketches from twenty seven architects. All plans were submitted to the Library Board and the City Council after careful examination a ballot was cast, each member writing on a card his choice. The plan of S.R. Badgley was selected (an old St. Catharines boy) when he was notified of our choice he came here and talked the matter over with the Library committee and notified us by letter he would make the plans as now sent you a free gift to the City ("for auld lang syne") . . . We advertised in three local papers and in the *Contractor and Builder* published in Toronto. In response we received three bids only . . . Owing to the bids being much higher than architects estimate the library committee finds itself in a quandary as to the best means of meeting the difficulty . . . Can you assist us by your valued advice and under all the existing circumstances would you supplement your very generous offer.[26]

The building was almost completed in December, 1904, when a new Mayor, A.W. Marquis, wrote to Bertram, explaining that while the building was substantially completed, funds had not been allocated for purchase of new furnishings:

Unfortunately the Library Board find that it will require $3,000 to furnish the interior in keeping with the building. This amount they lack, and with some hesitation on their part and on the part of the City Council, owing to your previous generosity, I have, at their request, been commissioned in pursuance of a resolution of our Council to ask if you would feel inclined to supplement your former gifts by this sum.[27]

Bertram did not. His answer a few days later was brief and to the point:

Mr. Carnegie considers that the amount he has already given was more than enough to erect a creditable and adequate Library Building for St. Catharines and he does not see his way to add to this amount.[28]

There is an interesting sidelight to this question of the furnishings. A week after Bertram's refusal was made known in the local newspaper, former mayor McIntyre, now a private citizen, wrote to Bertram saying how pleased he was that Carnegie had refused to entertain any further appeals for the Library. He explained that the lack of furnishings was the fault of City Council, who had totally ignored the Library Board in the planning and building of the Library, and that they should now bear responsibility for their lack of foresight.[29]

In any case, with new furnishings which may or may not have been paid for, the St. Catharines Carnegie Library opened on the afternoon of January 2, 1905, with the Nineteenth Regiment orchestra in full dress uniform providing a musical background for the 2,500 visitors.[30]

Procedures, problems and opposition

Carnegie grants for Ontario libraries would continue until 1917, with some requests honoured as late as 1923. As the table in Appendix 1 indicates, most years resulted in from two to eight or nine applications, with 1902 and 1911 producing the most: 12 and 15 respectively.

It should not be assumed, however, that procedures for receiving the grants became easier as the programme matured; on the contrary, Bertram attempted to formalize the procedures and he paid increasing attention to minute details of the information supplied by each community. The exact wording of resolutions, the official capacity of the correspondents, the type of plans sent for approval—as well as their contents—were all matters that concerned him.

The original questionnaire was expanded within a few years to ensure more detailed answers, since some communities were less than explicit in their responses, a factor which caused Bertram great difficulty. St. Thomas, for example, had answered the facility and support questions as follows:

Has it a Library at present: *Yes*
Amount Taxes Paid by Community Yearly for support:
about $1,156.00

Bertram's responding letter in February, 1906, indicated that he had expected more information.

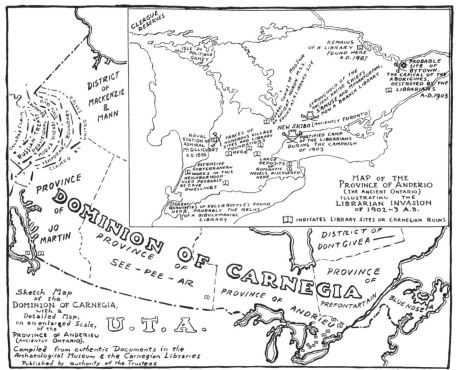

Carnegie Cartoon. *Opposition to the acceptance of a Carnegie grant was common in many communities, and the library building programme was frequently subjected to ridicule in local newspapers or magazines. This cartoon from* The Moon, *February 21, 1903, was typical of many that appeared at that time.*

Grand Valley Carnegie library. *Grand Valley had more difficulty than most communities in securing a Carnegie grant. They had problems with almost every aspect of the procedures, from the Questionnaire which the Carnegie Corporation required, to the building site, the architect's plans, and the maintenance pledge. Bertram complained, as well, about the extreme slope of the site and the extra building costs which such a slope would impose.*

41

Schedule of answers received. You give no particulars of the present accomodation nor of the income, disbursements, etc., of the Library.[1]

The second version of the questionnaire (shown in Appendix 2) included requests for information about book circulation, number and measurements of rooms in the existing library, and details of library financing. Even these questions, although much more specific, did not always produce the desired results for Bertram, and they certainly caused considerable difficulty for some communities. Grand Valley had particular trouble with Question 9:

Rate and amount at which Council will pledge support of Library yearly (levying tax for purpose) if building obtained.

Grand Valley Reeve James J. Reith, having had the questionnaire returned twice for being incomplete, finally wrote in desperation that "we are rather at sea to know just how you wish question 9 answered, and if you can enlighten us any would be very much pleased." Returning the Schedule of Questions for the third and last time, Bertram finally indicated that the Reeve had supplied the rate but not the amount which the Council was willing to pledge. With this explicit direction the Grand Valley Council successfully completed Question 9.[2]

The letter of promise, on which the Carnegie Corporation placed so much importance, also became standardized over the years. In December, 1909, the Ayr Library Board received this standard letter in response to their earlier request and completed questionnaire:

If the city agrees by resolution of council to maintain a Free Public Library at a cost of not less than Five Hundred Dollars a year, and provides a suitable site for the bilding, Mr. Carnegie will be glad to give Five Thousand Dollars to erect a Free Public Library for Ayr.[3]

Within two years that statement had been expanded to include another paragraph, as in this letter of promise to Forest Mayor E. Rumford, in May, 1911:

It should be noted that the amount indicated is to cover the cost of a Library Bilding complete, redy for occupancy and for the purpose intended. Before any expenditure on bilding or plans is incured, Mr. Carnegie's approval of proposed plans should be secured, to obtain which pleas send sketch plans for inspection.[4]

Later letters included an additional statement asking assurance that the building can be "erected complete, ready to occupy, and within the amount specified."

Upon receipt of the letter of promise the Town or City Council was expected to return a formal resolution, indicating compliance with the two conditions—provision of a suitable site and a guarantee of maintenance at the sum stated. Many communities had so much difficulty with the exact wording of such a resolution that Bertram standardized this as well. A sample resolution or pledge is included as Appendix 3.

Even with formalized procedures difficulties remained. For instance, Bertram was unwilling to provide a grant if he felt existing library facilities were adequate. Hamilton, which had constructed a library building in 1890, received the following request in response to their completed questionnaire in March, 1906. Bertram wrote: "Should like to see a picture of the building at present occupied as a Library, with plans showing all the accommodations."[5] After several exchanges about the floor plans, and with photographs and explanations supplied by Hamilton Library Board member J.N. Gibson, Bertram was still not sympathetic: "Yours of 22nd May and other correspondence has been before Mr. Carnegie this morning, but he does not think that the present Library Building has served its day and feels indisposed to replace it with a new building."[6]

At an impasse with these negotiations in 1906, it was not until 1909 that the Hamilton Library Board, with their new and determined librarian Adam Hunter, decided to renew their efforts to secure a Carnegie library. Hunter's first letter was turned down in Bertram's usual curt manner. "I enclose previous correspondence about your Library Building as it is useless to go over the same ground again with you. Please return when you are finished with it."[7]

Undaunted and uninvited, a deputation from the Hamilton Library Board went to New York in February, 1909, and although they failed to see either Carnegie or Bertram, they did manage to impress other officials of the Corporation with the validity of their case for a new library. A grant of $75,000 was made by Bertram in March of that same year, on condition that the City grant an additional $25,000 from the sale of the 1890 building. The Hamilton Council was expected to support the new library with at least ten per cent of the total cost of $100,000.[8]

Although the two conditions—purchase of a site and guarantee of ten per cent maintenance—were all that the Town or City Councils had to meet, objections to one or both of these conditions were raised in many communities. The choice of the site frequently became an obstacle, at least for some citizens. In Brussels, when the Town Council planned to convert the village market site into a library, a public petition was circulated and sent to Andrew Carnegie directly, objecting to the "high handed" measures of the Council. After another site was selected a second opposing petition was circulated. Bertram tartly replied to the petitioner's lawyer, A.H. Monteith, that "Mr. Carnegie deals with the community of Brussels through its elected representatives—Mayor and Council."[9]

In St. Marys, James Baxter as a private citizen wrote on behalf of a "large number of citizens and business men", asking Bertram to withhold the Carnegie grant until a new election would, it was hoped, get rid of the existing Council. The site chosen, he explained, belonged to a member of Council who hoped to increase the value of his property, and was, besides, described as "unsightly, surrounded by livery stables, cattle yards, and salt sheds." In the end, either a new Council or saner heads prevailed, for the present St. Marys Carnegie Library is well sited, on a lot adjacent to the Town Hall.[10]

A similar petition arguing against the grant acceptance was generated in Grand Valley by citizens who suspected that their Council was being less than honest with the Carnegie Corporation. Signed by fifteen local businessmen, the March 13, 1911 letter which accompanied the petition claimed that the Grand Valley Council had never raised the required one-half mill for library purposes and that "fraudulent means would have to be used to make up the necessary percentage required by the grant." Moreover, the petitioners stated that the Council had refused to give a site for the library, proposing instead "to buy an old

Hamilton Carnegie library. *Hamilton, like London, had difficulty
convincing Bertram that they should receive a building grant since they
already had a library building. A determined Library Board and Librarian
persuaded the Carnegie Corporation that Hamilton should be eligible and this
handsome library building was the result.*

Orillia Carnegie library. *The original Carnegie building in Orillia, shown
above, has been hidden by a modern addition of brick and glass.*

brick building in an out of the way place for $1,000. and use this old material in the new library, and by doing this Mr. Carnegie would really be paying for the site." However, a petition in favour of the grant was sent to Carnegie one week later, assuring him that the ratepayers of Grand Valley were "heartily in accord" with the proposed Library and that they fully realized "the benefits and advantages" such an institution would provide to their "prosperous little village." This second petition contained 134 signatures, including those of Library Board and Town Council members. It must have impressed the Carnegie Corporation favourably, since negotiations for the grant proceeded.[11]

In Orillia, similar differences of opinions arose. Opposition related to the amount of the maintenance pledge, which some citizens claimed would perpetually saddle the town with an unnecessary burden. More fervent, however, was the antagonism to Andrew Carnegie himself. A local newspaper, *The Orillia Times*, opened its columns to the opinions of citizens in March, 1909, and one correspondent, C.L. Stephens, wrote as follows:

> Should Orillia ask Mr. Andrew Carnegie for $10,000.00 to build a free public library? Most emphatically I think not. So far Orillia is a free and independent town, owing nothing to any special favor from any person or corporation outside of her own limits. We have all our churches, schools, Collegiate Institute, Y.M.C.A. building, public hospital, electric power, light and water supply, and Opera House, all paid for by the townspeople of Orillia in the shape of taxes or by private subscription. Having provided all these things for ourselves why should we now sink our independence by begging an unfriendly foreigner to give us of his ill-gotten gains, and at the same time tie a millstone around the necks of ourselves and our descendants for all time. Surely if an effort be made within the next few years there will be found money and public spirit enough in the town to provide a free public library of our very own, not burdened with the Carnegie name as a prefix. All the successful business of our town and our manufacturing establishments are in the hands of native born Canadians, or men born under the folds of the flag to which we are proud to owe allegiance, and surely the time will come when some of these gentlemen will be pleased and glad to perpetuate their name and successful business career by having it associated with the Free Public Library.[12]

The opposite viewpoint was expressed by J.E. Dickson a few days later:

> Shall we be behind other towns of far less merit than Orillia? Bracebridge has a Carnegie Library. Collingwood has one costing $15,000. Lindsay has one and so has each of a hundred other towns in Ontario. He then addressed himself to the question of accepting Carnegie money. 'Is it beneath us to accept money from such a source for such a purpose?' Wiser men than we have done so. Queen's University got $50,000 from Carnegie. Victoria got an equal sum. If we should so sin we should at least have the consolation that we do so in good company. Some would not accept because Carnegie's wealth was wrung from the hand of the poor man. 'It is blood money' some say. But is it? We have no evidence that such is the case. Many assert that Carnegie was not a hard taskmaster, and even if he were, is that sufficient reason why we should be willing to sacrifice the future of Orillia by refusing a good thing when it is within our grasp?[13]

Council must have agreed with the second writer for they voted to accept the grant, and were even prepared to increase maintenance to $1250 per annum to qualify for a larger grant.[14]

The phrase, 'blood money,' included in the Orillia debate, referred to the deaths which occurred during the 1892 strike at the Carnegie Steel Company in Homestead, Pennsylvania, and it caused some concern about accepting the building grants. For example, J.H. Elliot, Chairman of the Midland Library Board wrote in 1911 to the Citizens National Committee, New York, of which the Midland Public Library was a subscribing member, for advice because ". . . there has been a little bit of questioning among the laboring classes in regard to the story of the Homestead Riots, as to whether under such conditions they ought to accept the money . . . "[15] Frederick Lynch, secretary of the Committee, referred the problem to Bertram, suggesting that the Midland Board be sent a copy of a speech which Carnegie had made in Manchester, England during the summer of 1905, "in regard to accusations by Socialists and Labor agitating councillors," so that Midland's working men could have their suspicions allayed.[16]

Similar concerns were raised in other Ontario communities, including Toronto and Stratford. The Chairman of the Guelph Library Board, James Watt, felt it important to send Carnegie, in August 1905, a copy of a letter written by "a laboring man" to the editor of *The Evening Mercury* in support of Carnegie against his accusers:

> The writer is heartily sick of the contemptible slander he hears and reads in the press from day to day about Andrew Carnegie. On passing the free library, which is now nearing completion, the other day, I thought of the absurdity of people objecting to the acceptance of that money, and to such expressions as 'it is not his money,' 'it is blood money,' etc. . . . Blood money, forsooth! . . . when did Andrew Carnegie get blood money? If his employees could have got higher wages any other place they were at liberty to go there. Andrew Carnegie did not control the labor market, neither did he control the market for his products. He, like other people, was subject to the laws of competition. . . .[17]

Nor was organized labour, at least as represented by the American Federation of Labor, (AFL) concerned about acceptance of the Carnegie library gifts. Samuel Gompers, AFL President wrote to a Toronto labour leader and suggested that Carnegie "might put his money to a much worse act." He felt that it would be better to "accept his library, organize the workers, secure better working conditions and particularly reduction in hours of labor and then workers will have some chance and leisure in which to read books."[18]

In the majority of communities, however, there was little formal objection to the grants, and mention of what their neighbours had received was frequently given to Carnegie officials as justification for receiving similar support. The Town Clerk of Walkerton, J.H. Scott, wrote to Carnegie in 1910, pointing out that:

> This is the County Town of Bruce, with a population of 3,100 the largest in the County. You have already contributed to 3 Libraries in this County, viz: Kincardine, Port Elgin and Lucknow. Being the Judicial and Municipal Centre it is desired that a building be erected which will be worthy of the importance of the Town.[19]

Similarly, Wallaceburg Mayor D.H. Gordon began that town's first letter of request, in July 1901, "It has just occurred to me, seeing that you are so generous to many neighboring towns and cities, that you might assist us in establishing a Public Library in this town."[20] This reference to other Carnegie libraries was particularly true for those communities which sought to use Carnegie funds for public functions in addition to library related services. These efforts consistently met opposition from Bertram. Grand Valley Reeve James Reith was quite forthright, assuring Bertram that adding a second floor to the Library could be accomplished at virtually no extra cost. Upon seeing the plans Bertram responded that, while "Mr. Carnegie encouraged lecture rooms in his libraries, a hall, 70 ft. × 40 ft. is substantially a 'town hall' which will accommodate more than your whole adult population and is not a lecture room."[21] Not to be deterred by this explicit refusal, Reith cited several Carnegie libraries which had been completed with similar large halls:

Waterloo, top storey, all hall;
Stratford, large hall, top storey;
Galt, lecture room and classroom all top storey;
Berlin, large hall, top storey;
St. Catharines, large hall, top storey.[22]

Bertram was indifferent to this argument and efforts to secure a two storey library for Grand Valley were abandoned. A plan without the second storey, similar to that of Fergus, was put forward successfully a few years later.

Palmerston, which was among the earliest grant recipients, managed to secure accommodation for much more than library facilities, primarily because at that time, 1902, Bertram did not insist on personally approving all plans. Having originally received a promise of $6,000 the Town Council increased its request to $10,000, with assurance of the normal 10 per cent maintenance pledge. Unfortunately, even the expanded grant could not provide for completion of their rather large building, and in 1903, the mistake was made of asking for an additional $1500. Bertram refused, explaining that an increase of 40 per cent over the original grant of $6000 should have secured ample accommodation for a small place like Palmerston and he asked to see the plans. His reaction to these was immediate and angry. He wrote to Library Board Chairman, E.K. Brown, stating that had Carnegie seen the plans before making a payment he would have insisted on changes. Calling the Palmerston building plans "altogether lavish," he concluded that "it is a wrong use of the money altogether, which he gives for a Library Building, to use it in providing an auditorium actually larger than all the accommodation given to the Library."[23]

A more difficult situation arose in Lucknow in 1907, because Bertram discovered the true intent of the Library Board before all the funds had been granted and he wrote Board President John Murchison an accusatory letter:

What you have planned is not a Library Building but a structure with only about 20 per cent of the building devoted to strictly library purposes, the rest being public hall and council room. Mr. Carnegie did not offer to pay for a Town Hall . . . A Town Hall 56' × 50' to hold easily all the adult population of Lucknow was neither asked for nor promised.[24]

47

Palmerston Carnegie library. *The Palmerston Carnegie library was completed in 1903, before Bertram insisted on approval of the floor plans. Several municipal functions, in addition to the Library, were included in the building. A similar plan was used in Lucknow, except that the multi-purpose nature of the building was discovered before the grant had been finalized, and Bertram insisted that the Lucknow Village Council pay part of the building costs themselves.*

Lucknow Carnegie library.

With the building half completed and at an impasse because financial agent Franks stopped the funds, Reeve John Joynt travelled to New York in 1909 and he and Bertram reached a compromise. The grant was reduced from $10,000 to $7,500 and the Library, as planned, could be continued after the Lucknow Village Council agreed to pledge $2,500 of its own funds toward the building.[25]

Financial agent Franks became directly involved in the Hanover grant in similar fashion, and after seeing the floor plans in 1907 he criticized the "Public Hall, Board Room, Staff Office, Kitchen, Bed Rooms, Fire Engine Rooms and a number of other features we have never heard of being included in a Library Building."[26] Mayor W.A. Mearns was not prepared to back down, responding to Franks that "Mr. Carnegie had made grants for composite buildings" in other municipalities, naming Palmerston, Lucknow and Sault Ste. Marie. Franks referred the problem to Bertram, who was quite firm in refusing any funds. During the next three years the Hanover Council prepared a variety of proposals, sent a delegation to visit Bertram in New York, and had new plans drawn but it was finally realized that a Carnegie grant would not be available for other than a library building. In May, 1910, Town Clerk John Taylor wrote to Bertram explaining that Council was going ahead with building a municipal building, and that new plans for "a Library, separate and distinct from any other building" would now be obtained."[27]

After his experience with Palmerston, Lucknow and Hanover, Bertram became more realistic and forceful about grant requests from Ontario. In 1907 he responded to a Harriston request, saying that plans of the proposed building would be required, since "we find many Canadian towns are prone to erect what is supposed to be a Library Building, the main part of which is really a public hall and, in some cases, a municipal office."[28]

Grants and Pledges

Although Carnegie's philosophy for library giving indicated that small rather than large communities should acquire the grants, there was a size—roughly under 2,000 population—which was considered too small for proper maintenance of a library. The amount of money donated related to the size of the population at the time of the most recent census, and Bertram asked for detailed census information from any community about which he was uncertain. The standard award was calculated at approximately $2 per capita, but Bertram could be persuaded to ignore this guideline if sufficient and convincing argument was given. Only ten Ontario grants were for $5,200 or less, even though some thirty-two Ontario communities had populations considerably less than 2,000 at the time they received their grant promise. Population and grant size are given for each Ontario recipient in Appendix 1, and the grant information is summarized in Table 5. The ten smallest communities to receive grants are shown in Table 6.

To put matters into perspective it should be realized that the 1910 grant of $10,000 could be considered to be worth about $650,000 today. Using modern building standards, a library appropriate for a municipality of 10,000 people in 1984 should contain a minimum of 6,000 square feet and would cost approximately $600,000. Thus the Carnegie grants were,

Table 5 Grant size[1]

Size of grant $	No. of Communities	Size of grant $	No. of Communities
3,000	1	15,000–15,500	8
4,000– 4,900	1	16,000–16,500	2
5,000– 5,200	8	17,000–19,000	2
6,000– 6,400	5	20,000	2
7,000– 7,500	12	23,000–24,000	3
8,000– 8,800	11	25,000–27,000	8
10,000–10,900	26	30,000	1
11,000–11,500	2	40,000–50,000	3
12,000–12,500	6	100,000	2
13,000–13,500	3	275,000	1
14,000–14,500	4		

Table 6 10 smallest Ontario grant recipients[2]

Community	Population (at time of grant)	Grant $
Ayr	807	5,200
Stirling	848	5,000
Norwich	888	7,000
Teeswater	930	10,000
Glencoe	950	5,000
Grand Valley	1,000	8,000
Markdale	1,015	7,000
Stouffville	1,025	5,000
Milverton	1,025	7,000
Travistock	1,028	7,500

Teeswater Carnegie library.
Teeswater was the smallest Ontario community to receive a Carnegie grant. With a population of 930 (in 1905) which was well under the 2000 population which the Carnegie Corporation considered a minimum for library maintenance purposes, their grant of $10,000 was totally out of proportion to the size of the community, and Teeswater had difficulty in keeping their maintenance pledge.

50

by any measure, a very generous provision for library buildings.

Teeswater, because it was such a small community, at first despaired of receiving Carnegie support. Several letters were sent to Carnegie by town officials including the following from Library Board member James Gallagher in September, 1905:

Andrew Carnegie Esq.
Millionaire Founder of Libraries,
Scotland.

Dear Sir;

Teeswater is a neat little village of 1000 population largely Scotch in the County of Bruce and Province of Ontario Canada.

Could you assist the Library Board here to properly care for the literary tastes of the people by aiding them to the extent of possibly six thousand dollars towards building a Library Building in conformity with your regulations regarding these grand and wise benefactions of yours. . . .[3]

The letter drew the following response from Bertram: "Yours of September 6th received on Mr. Carnegie's return from Scotland. Mr. Carnegie does not think it advisable to put up a Library Building for 1000 people."[4] The return argument from Teeswater, similar to that of many other small communities, was that "although Teeswater's population is only about 1000, the combined population of this village and surrounding country which is served by the Library here is about as great as that of Lucknow and surrounding country which has just received favorable consideration at your hands."[5] Faced with reference to a familiar precedent (Lucknow had a population of 1111) Bertram withdrew his objections. The Teeswater Council persuaded him that they were quite capable of supporting a $1,000 annual levy, and the $10,000 grant was approved.

Berlin, of all Ontario communities, had the most luck in securing grants from the Carnegie Corporation. The town's first grant, for $15,000, was received in May, 1902, and additional grants of $4,000 (September, 1902) and $4,000 (April, 1903) were obtained before their building was formally opened in January, 1904. A fourth grant of $1500 was received in February, 1904 in order to complete the furnishing of the new library, making a total of $24,500 received for the initial building.[6]

By 1907 the Berlin Library Board realized that their library was inadequate, a situation which they blamed on their architect, Charles Knechtel, and his design of a stack room which was too small and a basement which was unusable due to high humidity. An application for $3500 to construct an addition was made to the Carnegie Corporation in 1908. Bertram replied sharply that "the financial affairs of this library at Berlin have been carried out in the most unsystematic, shortsighted and generally helpless manner of any of the 1920 which Mr. Carnegie has given."[7] Berlin Board member W.A. Bradley (who was also at that time President of the Ontario Library Association) defended the actions of the Board, explaining the problems they had experienced convincing the Council of the need for new furnishings; the necessity to proceed slowly in introducing library expenditures to the City; and finally providing detailed information about Berlin's rapid expansion as evidenced by the rising assessment base.

Bertram relented and the additional $3,500 was awarded in 1909.[8] However, by 1913 the building was again considered too small for the needs of the city of more than 15,000, and in spite of five previous grants having been received it was decided to have Mayor W.O. Euler request funds for an addition which would be sufficient to add two wings and a second stack floor. Support was gained from Walter R. Nursey, Ontario Inspector of Public Libraries, who wrote to Bertram in March, 1914 on behalf of the Berlin request. Referring to Berlin as growing very rapidly and "about to occupy a foremost place among the third class towns of the Province," Nursey asked that the Berlin request be considered without inflicting injustice upon other applicants.[9]

Bertram's response to Nursey was as direct—and negative—as his earlier letters to Berlin:

> . . . the Berlin bilding is one of the most short sitedly planned bildings of which I have seen the plans. It is cut up into small areas and the balcony feature could only have been introduced under the belief that money was no object as it is absolutely unnecessary and entails expenditure of money without any return whatever.[10]

The Berlin Council and Library Board were undaunted. W. H. Breithaupt, chairman of the Library Board Building Committee, travelled to New York in 1913 and was personlly interviewed by Bertram. Upon his return to Berlin he sent plans and elevations of the proposed addition, with cost estimates and assurance from the City that the library maintenance would be increased to cover the additional grant requested—$26,500. Bertram refused this request on the grounds of the poor design of the initial building and because he felt the city's population size simply did not warrant a bigger building. Nevertheless, after two more meetings with Bertram in New York and repeated letters submitting different and variously priced additions, Breithaupt was successful in persuading Bertram that a grant of $12,900 supplemented by $6,100 from the city, would be appropriate. Delayed for a year by the outbreak of war, Breithaupt wrote to inform Bertram of the commencement of work on the addition in the spring of 1915. After the Library's formal re-opening in February, 1916, and submission to the Carnegie Corporation of the required plans and photographs, Bertram sent an unusually gracious letter:

> I congratulate you on the fine send-off the enlarged library bilding obtained. You deserv great credit for bringing the matter to such a satisfactory conclusion, considering the sortcomings of the original bilding. The enlarged structure has a handsome and dignified appearance, judging by the newspaper picture, and I have no doubt that it is very satisfactory inside.[11]

Breithaupt's efforts on behalf of the Berlin (renamed Kitchener in 1916) Library did not end with the 1916 addition. From 1919 to 1922 he made repeated requests for a grant with which to re-excavate the original basement and convert it to a Story Hour Room and Auditorium, but he finally had to accept the fact that Carnegie grants for library construction were no longer available.

There is little doubt that the determination of one man, W. H. Breithaupt, was the primary factor in the successful grant applications which made the Berlin additions possible. Similar dedication by members of other communities can also be identified, most notably Judge A.D. Hardy of Brantford, James Bain and George Locke of Toronto, and Andrew Braid of Windsor.

Berlin Carnegie library, completed in 1903. *Berlin (now Kitchener) received more Carnegie grants than any other Ontario community. Bertram was particularly critical of the verandas on the 1903 building, calling them "wasteful."*

Berlin Carnegie library, after the 1916 addition. *The 1916 addition eliminated the verandas, and Bertram called the renovated library both "handsome and dignified."*

Several Ontario Communities began the process required to receive a Carnegie grant but failed to follow through for a variety of reasons, most frequently unwillingness on the part of Town Councils to pledge the support needed or to provide a suitable site. Included in the Carnegie Library Correspondence are requests and letters of promise for the communities shown in Table 7.

The *Report* of the Inspector of Public Libraries for 1909 indicates that seven additional communities, as in Table 8, had at that time been promised grants, although no reference of any sort exists in the Carnegie files.

Of the communities which did not complete the grant process and which are included in the Carnegie Library Correspondence, Tilbury had the most interesting—or frustrating—experience. A series of negotiations began in 1913 and continued until 1927, when Bertram wrote with some exasperation to Inspector of Public Libraries W. O. Carson that he estimated there were more than one hundred letters in the Tilbury file. Originally promised $5,000 for a Carnegie library in July, 1914, the Tilbury plans were finally approved by Bertram and went to tender in August, 1916. Unfortunately (but not untypically) all tenders came in considerably over the promised grant amount. In January, 1917 Bertram responded negatively to a request for an additional $2,000 by first stating that building materials could not have increased in cost by 40 per cent. Tilbury Town Clerk W.A. Hutton then asked Ontario Library Inspector Carson to intervene on their behalf, but Carson cautioned the community about promising more for maintenance (i.e. $700) than the legislation would allow them legally to raise. After more correspondence Bertram finally promised to raise the grant to $7,000, on condition that Tilbury levy the maintenance tax immediately, holding the first $100 for purchase of books. This the town pledged, and Franks was instructed to begin payments in July, 1918.

However, in August, 1918, H.H. Hallett, a new member of Council, wrote privately to Bertram, explaining that "there is great dissension among the citizens of Tilbury over the site chosen for the Carnegie Library. Suffice it to say the site chosen is on a short side street upon which the Reeve and the Clerk of the town reside and is immediately behind a general store in which the Mayor is heavily interested." Calling this situation "rotten," Hallett revealed a more fundamental problem: Tilbury had never officially passed the bylaw required by the Public Libraries Act to qualify their library as free and public—a Carnegie grant condition.

Bertram advised consulting the Inspector of Public Libraries once again, and he sent the inflammatory Hallett letter to the Town Council. Town Clerk W.A. Hutton, responded "that the Council of the Town of Tilbury is composed not of crooks," but Carson further explained that their actions were indeed illegal until a bylaw had been formally passed. Moreover, the Libraries Act only permitted a tax-rate of one half a mill on existing assessment, which would not raise $350 a year in Tilbury let alone the required $700.

Although Tilbury eventually did pass the necessary bylaw creating a free public library, Bertram's stipulation of $700 maintenance could not be satisfied in spite of a variety of suggestions including the town providing free gas for heating. Bertram therefore withdrew the grant in February 1919. A further change in the Public Libraries Act in 1921 made it possible, however, for Tilbury to secure the necessary maintenance funds and negotiations commenced anew, with Tilbury claiming that labour costs after the war were now delaying procedures. Bertram reminded Tilbury that the promise was now "seven years and four months

Plaque honouring Judge A.D. Hardy, Brantford. *Many of the Ontario grants would not have been realized had it not been for the dedication of a few individuals.*

Table 7   Rejected applications[12]

Community	Population	Date of application	Grant promised $
Caledonia	952	1911	6,000
Gananoque	3804	1912	10,000
Millbank	793	1913	8,000
Otterville	2271	1915	6,000
Tilbury	704	1914	5,000

Table 8 Additional (rejected) applications[13]

Community	Amount of grant $
Arthur	7,500
Merrickville	2,500
Paisley	5,000
Petrolia	10,000
Port Arthur	30,000
Strathroy	7,500
Thessalon	8,000

old and the war had been over over three years" but in January, 1922 he once again instructed Franks to begin payments to Tilbury. Still the building did not materialize, this time, according to Mayor E.G. Odette, because it was "blocked consistently by a few discontented citizens." At the request of Inspector Carson, Tilbury Town Clerk C.E. Stevenson informed Bertram in December, 1924, that it would be impossible "to erect a suitable building at this time." The grant was formally withdrawn. Writing to Bertram in 1927 Carson spoke with regret of the problems that Tilbury had experienced, and mentioned that although "he had very little sympathy with that town, due to the fights . . . the warring parties of some time ago had left Tilbury."[14] It is unfortunate that they had not left earlier!

Most of the grants refused were usually those requesting additions: Stratford, Windsor, and Thorold all unhappily fell into this category. Typical of these refusal letters was that to St. Thomas Board Chairman Witt Murel in April, 1913:

> The amount alredy allowed for library bilding for St. Thomas is as much as is given for a place with its population . . . We do not consider it feasible to add to the present building which is not advantageously shaped nor laid out to the best advantage.[15]

Those communities which did not formally seek Carnegie grants make for as interesting a study as those which did. Typical was the case of flourishing London. In his 1906 Report, Inspector for Public Libraries T.W.H. Leavitt incorporated photographs, floor plans and brief descriptions of modern public libraries of Ontario. Included was a report from the London Public Library, which had a building completed in 1895 and enlarged in 1903. In addition to the comments on material, costs, heating systems, and so on, was the following proud statement: "Have had no gifts from Mr. Carnegie. No steps have been taken or will be taken to secure any."[16] The passage of half-a-dozen years saw a change of opinion. The Minutes of the February 6, 1913 meeting of the London Public Library Board include a notice of motion that: "The Board apply to Andrew Carnegie, Esq. for a sum of money for the purpose of building and furnishing a new library building. . . ."[17]

At subsequent meetings it was agreed that a grant of $125,000 should be sought, and negotiations were begun with Bertram. Citing Hamilton as an example to be followed (owing to their similar circumstance of possessing a relatively new library building) the London Board found that Bertram proved difficult with respect to the value of their existing building. It was therefore agreed that the Board Chairman Dr. James Ross, accompanied by Dr. A.O. Jeffrey, a Board member, would travel to New York to discuss the difficulty with either Bertram or Carnegie.

Unfortunately events were overtaken by tragedy. In New York on November 18, 1913, prior to meeting with Carnegie, Ross went "to visit a favourite old bookshop . . . A heavy man and somewhat hard of hearing, he stepped from behind a trolley car into the path of an automobile."[18] He died, almost instantly. The London Board was so dispirited by this incident that further attempts to secure a Carnegie library for London were abandoned.

As has been noted, each community that received a grant was required to submit a pledge in the form of a resolution guaranteeing annual maintenance of the library at not less than 10 per cent of the gift amount. Ontarians had diverse opinions regarding the validity of this pledge. It was not unusual for a Council or Board member to write to an acquaintance in a similar capacity in another community and inquire about procedures for securing a grant as well as conditions for the pledge. A response to such a letter, addressed to Board Member Hal Donly of Simcoe from Listowel Mayor F.W. Hay, gives one opinion:

> I will give you below what information I have in regard to our Carnegie Library . . . No doubt if you get this grant you will receive from Mr. Franks a form to fill out and sign, but I do not remember that we even had to do this, and I do not believe either that the resolution of the Council of this year holds or binds the following Councils.
>
> I suppose what you are most anxious about is to learn if they make you live up strictly to the ten per cent expenditure. I might say that our Library has been up four years, and we have never heard from Mr. Carnegie in any way, and I am quite satisfied he does not know whether we are spending ten dollars a year or one thousand dollars to maintain it. . . .[19]

Minutes of the Fergus Library Board for June 1, 1909, reveal another opinion, with a report by a Board member of an encounter at an Ontario Library Association meeting held that year in Berlin:

> In conversation with Mr. Nursey, Inspector of Libraries, he has formed the opinion that Mr. Carnegie, being a fair man, did not intend living strictly to the line; that Mr. Carnegie's wish is that a library endowed by him shall be efficiently maintained and that the 10 per cent basis merely means efficient maintenance.[20]

Notwithstanding these strong opinions in Ontario, the Carnegie Corporation was, as we have seen, most keenly interested in strict adherence to the maintenance pledge, and as early as 1914 Bertram attempted to ensure that the pledge requirements were being met. For this purpose he worked closely with the Inspectors of Public Libraries in Toronto, and a December, 1916 letter to Inspector Carson reflects his views on the pledges:

> In regard to the difference between the amounts which Tavistock and Teeswater ar under the law able to provide for carrying on their libraries and the amounts which they voluntarily and specifically contracted to provide in order to obtain the library buildings, I hav to state that in each case an official application was made with the distinct statement that $750 a year and $1,000 a year respectively wer to be provided from taxation for carrying on the library . . . This Corporation could not proceed on the assumption that elected officials of communities in Canada, or elsewhere, would make false statements on the one hand or do not know the law under which they liv on the other. The issue is not one of this Corporation being too generous, but your statement puts these two communities in the position of having falsely stated that they would levy a tax to produce $750 and $1,000 a year respectively to obtain donations they did receiv.[21]

Bertram recognized that the pledges had no legal basis, as a later communication to the Tillsonburg Board Chairman, W.C. Brown, indicated. "Acceptance of a pledge by Tillsonburg or any other town was a matter of good faith rather than insistence upon legal form. The pledge is sufficiently indicative of what Mr. Carnegie's intentions were and what Tillsonburg undertook to do."[22]

Bertram continued his attempts to rectify pledge irregularities through the Inspector of Libraries. In 1917 Inspector Carson wrote, for example, to the Secretary of the Dresden Public Library: "The Carnegie corporation has made a very strong protest to the Minister of Education regarding a few libraries that have failed to keep their pledges, and they threaten to take drastic means against the libraries, including publicity for lack of faith."[23] An earlier letter, which he asked to be read aloud to the Board, stated:

> . . . I am indeed sorry to note that you failed to keep faith with the Carnegie Corporation. They have complained to the Minister . . . Although the Department is no parent to the pledge we are interested. The Corporation says that it will not make grants until the few libraries who have broken their pledges begin to keep their agreements . . .
>
> Do try to keep your pledge with the Carnegie Corporation . . . I have seen the pledges and I cannot understand how any library could pledge its honour and treat the matter lightly. We feel very keenly the disgrace that some of the libraries have cast upon us.[24]

Another problem which arose was the number of communities which, having been given a grant for a Carnegie library building, began within a few years to use their library for other purposes. Not infrequently this led to letters of concern addressed to either Carnegie or Bertram. Typical is the following from the Hanover Library Board in February, 1914:

> The Council of the Town of Hanover last year opened this basement [of the Library] for dancing parties and permitted all kinds of people to hold dances there, lately the people attending these dances bring Whiskey with them and cause considerable disturbance . . . Now I wish to know, does Mr. Carnegie approve of turning this Library into a dance hall, we strongly object to doing so, and we believe a letter from Mr. Carnegie would settle the matter.[25]

Bertram responded that "any use of the building for other than purposes connected with the library is not keeping faith with the sense of the request and the promise which was made in response to the request."[26] Moreover, he wrote to Inspector Carson: "I haven't kept any statistics, but it seems to me there is in your territory considerable flouting of the good faith which should characterize the use of these buildings."[27] Carson and Bertram were not able to ensure adherence to the spirit of the pledges, and private citizens or Library Board members from many rural Ontario communities continued to turn to the Carnegie Corporation for assistance in forcing their Town Councils to honour the pledges. The Secretary of the Harriston Library Board wrote in 1919 that "I would like to see the Council uphold the town's honour and am ready to do anything I can to have them fulfil the contract that was made with your Corporation."[28] As recently as 1940 requests for assistance in enforcing the pledges were still being received, and the following letter to Grand Valley in May, 1940 was typical of the Carnegie Corporation's view:

> Your letter of May 1, addressed to the late James Bertram, has come to me for reply. Mr. Carnegie and Carnegie Corporation succeeding him in his library work, as a matter of policy never participated in the management of libraries in buildings provided by Carnegie funds. It should be realized that a request was made for a *library*

Dresden Carnegie library. *Dresden received a Carnegie grant of $8000 in 1906, but by 1917 had failed to fulfill their pledge of support for the library. The Dresden Public Library Board was severely chastised by the Ontario Public Library Inspector for this dereliction of duty.*

Portraits by Moonlight.

Carnegie cartoon. *A contemporary caricature of Andrew Carnegie appeared in several Canadian newspapers or magazines during the building grant programme. This sketch is from the February 21, 1903 issue of* The Moon.

building, and relying on the good faith of the community, money was provided for a free public library building. For any part of the building to be used for other than library purposes would it seems to us, be contrary to the original understanding.[29]

This lack of commitment to keeping the pledges, both for maintenance and use of the library buildings, as will be shown, was in part responsible for the termination of the building grants by the Carnegie Corporation in 1917.

Carnegie, Bertram and the Inspectors of Public Libraries

Although James Bertram was clearly the key figure in the Carnegie library philanthropy in Ontario, the records show a few direct links with Andrew Carnegie. As well, the Ontario Department of Education, through its Inspectors for Public Libraries, became, as noted, intimately involved with the process, more particularly as controls and validation of eligibility became necessary.

As observed earlier, Carnegie personally opened the Ottawa Carnegie Library on April 30, 1906. Arriving in Canada's capital in a private railway car attached to the "Toronto train" on Saturday, April 28, he spent three days as the guest of Governor General Earl Grey at Government House.[1] An observer among the crowd that greeted him at the train station was impressed with his appearance:

> A little old gentleman much below the average in stature, for he doesn't seem over five feet high; a short broad face, portraying lines of Scottish character and illumined by a pleasant smile; a neatly trimmed beard, almost snowy in its whiteness; a pair of snappy blue eyes; a quiet, conventional attire—plain blue overcoat, tweed trousers and a common-place Derby—and over all a happy expression, such is Andrew Carnegie, multi-millionaire, philanthropist, steel king of Pittsburg, laird of Skibo Castle.[2]

There was considerable interest in Carnegie's visit prior to his arrival, and poems of welcome were printed in *The Saturday Evening Citizen*. A few verses from one, by "Libraria," are repeated below:

> To Mr. Andrew Carnegie
>
> Welcome, Mr. Carnegie
>
> Welcome for your own true worth,
> To our fair city of the North.
>
> Son of Dunfermline, over the sea,
> Patron of arts and industry,
> From Saxon, Frenchman, Celtic clan
> Welcome true Cosmopolitan
>
> . . . .
>
> And happy be your stay, though brief,
> Where British flag and Maple Leaf,
> Beneath our spring-time skies of blue,
> Are waving welcomes glad for you.[3]

This was an appropriate prelude to the address which Carnegie gave that Saturday evening to the Canadian Club at "Russell house." Greeted with "three cheers and a Tiger" he informed his audience that Canada owed its "proud position to the United States, which had refused to relinquish one iota of fiscal independence for empire." He praised the example provided by Canada and America for "peace among nations," and "the open pathways of peaceful communication between the two branches of our race here on the North American continent." Noting Sir Wilfrid Laurier in the audience, Carnegie admitted that he was "a race imperialist" but, calling Laurier one of the five greatest men in the world, "he included the French all the time," and that France, Great Britain and America were a powerful alliance for world peace.[4]

On Sunday Carnegie visited the federal government experimental farm, expressing admiration for the work of the Improvement Commission. A special dinner that evening included Robert Borden, Mackenzie King and Wilfrid Campbell as guests.[5] On Monday, before he left with Sir Sandford Fleming for the Library opening at three o'clock, he was "taken by surprise." Fleming, who was Chancellor of Queen's University, had arranged to have Principal D.M. Gordon available to assist him in presenting the diploma and hood, emblematic of the degree of LL.D. 'in honoris causa,' conferred upon Carnegie by Queen's University a few weeks previously. Also present was Dr. Nicholas Murray Butler, President of Columbia University, who, with James Bertram and two other friends, had accompanied Carnegie to Canada.[6]

The Library opening was attended by "a large crowd which blocked Metcalfe Street in their anxiety to get a glimpse of the little man from Skibo."[7] The Mayor thanked Carnegie on behalf of the City, commenting that it seemed fitting to emphasize that "in broadening the scope of his philanthropy to include both the mother country and the King's dominions beyond the seas he was contributing to the friendly alliance between the British empire and the United States which would be in the interest of world peace." Carnegie responded by saying how pleased he was to visit Canada "and see for myself our northern neighbour, in which the Scottish element has been from the first." Before declaring the Library officially open he explained why he considered public libraries, free to the people, so beneficial and hoped that they would spread throughout the Dominion.[8]

During his tour of the Library, which followed the formal ceremony, Carnegie was again surprised by an unscheduled ceremony: the Ottawa St. Andrew's Society chose the stock room for their presentation of a formal address of welcome. Before he left the building to say "a few friendly words to the people waiting on the steps outside" he congratulated the Library architect, E.L. Horwood, for a "magnificent structure." He then departed in a carriage to the sound of "rousing cheers."[9]

Carnegie had spent the day before his arrival in Ottawa in Toronto, "automobiling, receiving deputations, meeting prominent men and visiting at the Grange, the residence of Mr. Goldwin Smith."[10] In the evening he addressed the Toronto Canadian Club with a speech almost identical to the one he delivered the next evening in Ottawa.

One of the brief stops on his city tour was at the Public Library (then at Adelaide and Church Street)[11] where he was thanked by the Library Board for a promised grant (see below). He also received a deputation on a similar mission from Victoria College.[12] As he left the Library he shook hands with "a group of ladies, members of the library staff, who were lined up to see him."[13] He was then taken to City Hall to receive an address of welcome by Mayor Emerson Coatsworth, and he responded by talking briefly about libraries and what he felt Toronto should be doing with the building grant which had been promised:

> I do not wish to interfere in the selection of sites or in the class of building you desire to put up. The money is yours, but I would have many branch libraries. I do not care about it being near universities, or colleges; these institutions have mostly all the books they need. I want the branch libraries to be near the people. I want them to attract the young, for young men may go to other objectionable places if the libraries are not convenient. The building should look quiet, dignified and classic, but not mere architectural structures. I am not going to put my hand in a hornets' nest by interfering with the architects, but my ideas of a library building are as I have stated and I am desirous that the branch libraries be as numerous as possible.[14]

A visit to the Smiths Falls Library was also part of Carnegie's first Canadian tour, although this took place only because of the extraordinary persistence of the Smiths Falls Library Board. Their first letter to Carnegie on the subject was sent in March, 1906:

> I write to extend an invitation to you to come to Smith's Falls on your approaching visit to Canada. We have built what is said to be the handsomest and most complete small library in the Province with the money so kindly given us by you and we would very much like the pleasure of showing it to you. I notice you go from Ottawa to Toronto. To do so you must needs pass through Smith's Falls and we would esteem it a great honor as well as a pleasure to have you stay here for even a few hours.[15]

A courteous but negative response came from Bertram:

> Mr. Carnegie tenders his thanks for your kind invitation to visit Smith's Falls and see the Library on his approaching visit to Canada. Mr. Carnegie regrets that the few days he will be in your country will be so fully taken up that it will be impossible for him to take advantage of your kind offer, but he begs to send his best wishes for the prosperity of the Smith's Falls Library and the happiness of all the people.[16]

But the Board wrote again, assuring Carnegie that he would be "picked up at the train, delivered back again and in all ways looked after," and he consented to come. The Smiths Falls Board minutes record that "A. Carnegie went through the new building from top to bottom, was delighted with it, and declared it a first prize library, and the handsomest small library he had seen of all that he had given." *The Rideau Record*, for May 1, 1906, reported that Carnegie was driven to the Library accompanied by his private secretary, Bertram, and was shown over every part of it. Moreover:

> He showed the most unaffected pleasure with everything. He thought it was a beautiful site and he was as genuinely pleased with the library as the proverbial boy is supposed to be with a new top. He said we had got more for our money than any building he had ever seen in his life that was built in the regular way without labor or material being contributed, and he further said we had the handsomest small library he had ever seen. In connection with this it might

Ottawa Carnegie library. *The Ottawa Public Library was the only Ontario Carnegie Library which the philanthropist opened in person. Andrew Carnegie spent three days in Ottawa in April 1906, as guest of the Governor General, Earl Grey, and seemed delighted at the great crowd present for the official library opening.*

Smiths Falls Carnegie library. *Carnegie stopped off to visit this library on his way to the opening of the Ottawa library in April 1906. It was the first of the Canadian Carnegie libraries which he had visited, and he called it the handsomest small library he had ever seen.*

be said that Smith's Falls had the honor of showing him the first library that he had seen in Canada. He had seen many of the libraries that he had given in the United States but this is his first visit to Canada and ours was the first library he had seen in this country . . . On the mantel in the reading room of the library there was a photograph of him in a frame. He noticed it and offered to put his autograph on it. In an instant it was out of the frame and borrowing a pen he wrote: 'A rare pleasure to visit a library I have given. Success to Smith's Falls.'[17]

St. Catharines was not so lucky. A request for a visit to their Library (at the time of the 1906 tour) met with the more usual response: "Mr. Carnegie tenders his grateful thanks for your kind invitation of March 17th and regrets that his engagements already make it impossible for him to accept, much as he would like to do so."[18] And a similar letter went from Bertram on behalf of Carnegie to Mayor H.A. Stonehouse of Wallaceburg in 1907:

Mr. Carnegie tenders his thanks for your kind invitation to be present at the opening of the Library and exceedingly regrets that it is impossible for him to be present. He begs to send his best wishes for the progress of the Library movement and the success and happiness of all the people of Wallaceburg.[19]

Sometimes unusual requests were made. It is hard to believe that a community would consider the following situation appropriate for Carnegie support, but a Forest physician, J.B. Hubbard, wrote in evident sincerity to Franks in December, 1912:

There is, however, an unfortunate case arising directly from the opening of the new library, to which we would draw your attention as we believe the relief needed has [not] been provided. At any rate you will know whether the case comes within the wide range of Mr. Carnegie's benevolences.

Miss V. Bradbury, aged about seventy, for twenty-one consecutive years librarian of the free library in this town lost her position with its small income from the opening of the new Carnegie library, and is now entirely dependent upon the bounty of her friends, which is intermittent and unsatisfactory and besides humiliating in its openness. It would take very little in the way of a pension to smooth her way and we would be greatly pleased to hear from you that something could be done, and to assist in any way possible.[20]

A few days later a reply was received from Bertram which indicated that the letter had been forwarded to him but that "Mr. Carnegie is unable to consider your application."[21]

Carnegie could be moved to a personal response, however, on some occasions. In March 1919, a Miss Belle Wilkerson wrote to Bertram from New Orleans, Louisiana, thanking Carnegie for his kindness in placing a library in "Picton, Canada." She mentioned that she had left Picton 35 years previously, but had visited her brother there in 1910, had been shown the new Library, and informed that "now the poor can read as well as the rich." Miss Wilkerson received the following in reply, signed by Andrew Carnegie himself, although he seemed not to realize which country Picton was a part of: "I am deeply touched by your kind letter of twelfth March which Mr. Bertram has forwarded to me. Such words of appreciation as yours more than compensate for the contributions it

Woodstock Carnegie library portico

Woodstock Carnegie library

Interior of Woodstock rotunda

Watford Carnegie library

Elmira Carnegie library showing part of a later addition

An unusual portico, Durham Carnegie library

Listowel Carnegie library

Seaforth Carnegie library

Smiths Falls Carnegie library

Smiths Falls light fixture

Smiths Falls original chair and hardware

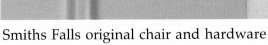

Campbellford Carnegie library with renovated portico

Mitchell Carnegie library, a red brick replica of Listowel

Hanover Carnegie library

Weston Carnegie library, now part of Metropolitan Toronto

Pembroke Carnegie library

Wychwood Branch, Toronto with recent addition on the right

Norwood Carnegie library

Forest Carnegie library

Galt Carnegie library seen across the Grand River

Brantford Carnegie library rotunda

Brantford Carnegie library

Shelburne Carnegie library

St. Marys Carnegie library

Watford Carnegie library

Riverdale Branch, Toronto

Picton Carnegie library

Goderich Carnegie library

has been my privilege to make to library work in the United States."[22]

The City of Hamilton also received one of Carnegie's rare personal letters, dated April 23, 1913. The expression of his philosophy and compliments to the City softened his rejection of the Board's invitation to visit the new Library:

It is with deep regret that I am compelled to admit the impossibility of being with you at the opening of the library, owing to numerous other engagements, St. Louis, Washington etc. I shall be busy until the day of our sailing for our usual holiday on the heather hills. I have seen Hamilton more than once. Coming home from Arkansas last Spring we purposely came through your section to get a glimpse of the Falls, and I stood at the rear end of the car and took a lingering look at Hamilton before any of you were up.

There is no question about Hamilton's future as a Manufacturing City, and it gives me inexpressible pleasure to know that I have contributed something to its success in one indispensible feature, a Public Library, free to all the people.

Confucius gave the world one of its great truths 'There being education there can be no distinction of classes.' Canada and the Republic can boast that any man's privilege in the State is every man's right. That insures peace, happiness and prosperity—above all it is simple justice—The man's the goud for a' that.

Deeply regretting my absence, but predicting that the Public Library and branches to come will prove wells from which only blessed waters will flow, and with special congratulations to the Scottish element in your midst, to which Hamilton owes so much.[23]

Contrary to public opinion, Carnegie did not insist that there be any recognition of his philanthropy in the library buildings, although he was obviously pleased when such recognition or similar honours spontaneously were accorded him. A room in his Scottish home, Skibo Castle, was decorated with carvings of the coats of arms from the British cities which had awarded him official freedom.[24] Ontario communities were also anxious to recognize their benefactor in some way; most did so by hanging a portrait over the reading room fireplace.

In the early years of the grant programme a photograph was sent to a corresponding community without charge. Picton's request was answered in February, 1908: "Mr. Carnegie tenders his thanks for the appreciative resolution . . . and has much pleasure in sending you his picture as requested."[25] By 1924 the pictures were no longer free. Guelph and Renfrew were referred to a dealer, as follows: "In reply to your inquiry I have to state that you can obtain a photograph of Mr. Carnegie, either large or small size, from Messers. Davis & Sanford, 597 Fifth Ave., New York."[26]

This standard photograph did not satisfy everyone. W. H. Breithaupt of Berlin mentioned that City's plan for a suitable memorial in a postscript to a 1916 letter to Bertram. "Incidentally, I may add that I looked up portraits of Mr. Carnegie at Davis and Sandfords' in New York and found that we could practically do as well by getting an enlargement here of the photograph kindly sent us by Mr. Carnegie's private secretary. This we have done and have quite a satisfactory picture."[27]

Hamilton found another alternative to the standard portrait, as a 1911 letter to Bertram from the Deputy Registrar, County of Wentworth, reveals:

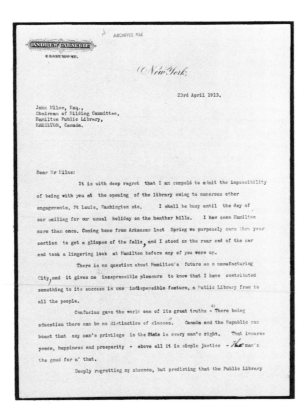

ANDREW CARNEGIE
2 EAST 91ST ST.

New York.

23rd April 1913.

John Milne, Esq.,
Chairman of Bilding Committee,
Hamilton Public Library,
HAMILTON, Canada.

Dear Mr Milne:

It is with deep regret that I am compeld to admit the impossibility of being with you at the opening of the library owing to numerous other engagements, St Louis, Washington etc. I shall be busy until the day of our sailing for our usual holiday on the heather hills. I have seen Hamilton more than once. Coming home from Arkansas last Spring we purposely came thru your section to get a glimpse of the falls, and I stood on the rear end of the car and took a lingering look at Hamilton before any of you were up.

There is no question about Hamilton's future as a manufacturing City, and it gives me inexpressible pleasure to know that I have contributed something to its success in one indispensible feature, a Public Library free to all the people.

Confucius gave the world one of its great truths - "There being education there can be no distinction of classes. Canada and the Republic can boast that any man's privilege in the State is every man's right. That insures peace, happiness and prosperity - above all it is simple justice - The man's the goud for a' that.

Deeply regretting my absence, but predicting that the Public Library

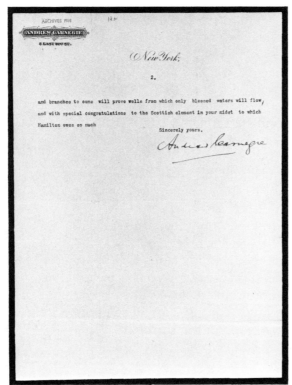

ANDREW CARNEGIE
2 EAST 91ST ST.

New York.

2.

and branches to come will prove wells from which only blessed waters will flow, and with special congratulations to the Scottish element in your midst to which Hamilton owes so much

Sincerely yours,

Andrew Carnegie

Letter from Andrew Carnegie. *One of the few letters sent directly from Andrew Carnegie, rather than from his secretary, James Bertram, was received by the City of Hamilton.*

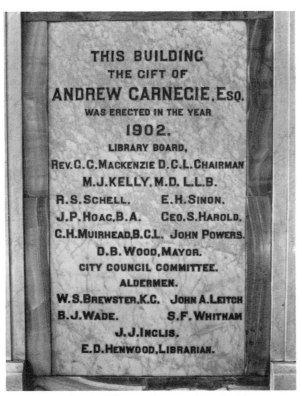

Carnegie plaque, Brantford. *Plaques honouring the donor were common features in the Ontario libraries.*

Bust of Andrew Carnegie. *This bust of Andrew Carnegie is a copy from the original by Sculptor Massey Rhind. It was commissioned in 1911 by the Hamilton Public Library Board to recognize their benefactor.*

In connection with our proposed new Library it has always been understood that some recognition of Mr. Carnegie's generosity should be made, and it had been practically agreed that this should be in the form of a brass tablet.

When in New York recently I had the pleasure of visiting Mr. Massey Rhind and of seeing replica of the bust of Mr. Carnegie made by him. I brought back with me a photograph of it and in showing it to members of the Board they thought it might answer our purpose and perhaps be not more expensive than the tablet, which was to have been specially designed; and subject of course to our ascertaining Carnegie's views in the matter the Board have agreed to substitute a copy of this bust in bronze for the original idea of a tablet.[28]

Bertram must have supported this idea, for the handsome bronze bust of Carnegie became a noted attraction in the Hamilton Carnegie Library and has been given a place of honour in the new Hamilton Library.

The relationship between Carnegie and Bertram, and their involvement in the Ontario grant programme, appears to have been understood at an early stage. *The Gazette* (Tavistock) for February 5, 1903, contained the following cryptic comment:

Andrew Carnegie goes on offering libraries to towns in Canada. In some cases the offers are accepted and in some cases not. In case of a refusal we wonder if the library-giver feels somewhat sat on. It is more likely that Carnegie knows only of the offers accepted, his secretary doing the offering.[29]

Although close friends described him as sympathetic and humorous, James Bertram, as reflected in his letters to the Ontario libraries, did not appear to be either warm or patient.[30] His response to a request for a personal interview was most frequently a curt refusal, as in the case of Hanover: "Mr. Carnegie does not give interviews about Library matters. There is nothing about a Library which cannot be arranged by correspondence."[31] To Town Clerk W.H. Smith of Ingersoll, who had requested that a School of Technical Training be included in their proposed Library, he simply wrote: "The answer to yours of March 22nd is in the negative."[32] Bertram was equally unsympathetic to requests that would provide decoration or some artistic pretension to the library interior. The Chairman of the Penetanguishene Library Board, J.B. Jennings, wrote inquiring if a mural, depicting historic events related to Penetanguishene, could be added to the Library. A list from which Bertram could choose an appropriate subject was forwarded to him, and included among other historical figures:

Governor Simcoe and the five Indian Chiefs signing at Penetanguishene a preliminary treaty of purchase of the land for the British Crown, in 1793.

The naval officers and marines towing the captured American warships, the *Scorpion* and the *Tigress* into the Penetanguishene Harbour in order to sink them (War of 1812-1814).[33]

Bertram's brief response: "Yours of March first receivd, the anser to which is in the negativ."[34]

This was not, however, his shortest message to an Ontario community. Due to his absence at Skibo Castle, Scotland, during a crucial part, to them at least, of the planning process, Ingersoll Town Clerk

W.H. Smith resorted to a telegram to hasten the approval of library plans. His message: "Waterloo, Ontario plans adopted for Ingersoll Carnegie Library. Cable if acceptable to you," was answered by Bertram: "Can't say without seeing."[35]

Bertram could also lose patience with a Town Clerk or Board if he had to spend too much time persuading them to revise their plans. A postscript to a letter to Exeter Library Board Secretary, H.E. Huston, suggests his exasperation:

> P.S. Do not refer to plans which "we wish" as if you were doing anything under compulsion. Try and adjust your mind to the fact that we hav had experience in these things and take advantage of that experience. Study the matter thorolly and see if it is not best for your community and that we ar likely to kno what is the best that can be had for the money.[36]

But nowhere can Bertram's exasperation with an Ontario community be better illustrated than with his own description of his experience with Thorold. Writing in 1911 he described Mayor McCulloch's most recent letter as:

> A climax to the loose and incapable way in which the authorities of Thorold hav handled this Library Bilding matter from the beginning. Eleven years ago, at the request of Thorold, Mr. Carnegie agreed to provide $10,000 for a bilding. Later he was askt to provide $6000, insted of $10,000, then $7000 insted of $6000 then back to $10,000, and after going thru all the trouble of adjusting the complications of this correspondence, you tell us not $10,000 but $13,000 is required to cover the cost of the building. Of course it is safe to say that this is an underestimate, rather than an overestimate.[37]

Bertram was not above chastising communities which did not honour the pledges which they made, either with respect to the floor plans which had been approved or the maintenance support. Kenora evidently deviated from the building plans on which grant approval had been based, a fact that Bertram discovered when he received the photographs of the completed building. He wrote suggesting that Kenora was ungracious. Defending the plan changes Kenora Board Chairman J.W. Humble explained that "we never get a building erected in this country without extras cropping up,"[38] and Bertram replied: "That comment on your general experience has no bearing on the present situation in view of the explicit pledge given, and, if you will pardon me for saying so, in the face of the pledge your statement shows a lack of a sense of responsbility."[39]

When funds which he considered unnecessary were requested Bertram could show his Scottish origins. Stouffville received approval for a $5,000 building in 1913, but the project had been suspended because of the war. When they asked to have the promise renewed in 1919 they also asked to have the grant doubled. Bertram's reply included a lesson in economics:

> If action had been taken by Stouffville with reasonable promptitude, the library building could have been erected at normal or even subnormal prices, so that it is fair to say that the expenditure of $10,000 now would not secure much more, if any more, than $5,000 would have secured then; thus this Corporation would simply be bearing the cost of the dilatoriness of your community.[40]

Penetanguishene Carnegie library. *The Penetanguishene Library Board asked for an additional grant of $2000 to be used for a mural depicting historical events relevant to their community. Bertram refused the request.*

Kenora Carnegie library. *When Bertram discovered what was in his view an unnecessary veranda on the rear of this library, he called the Kenora Library Board "ungracious."*

The Library Board in Waterloo was also criticized because they asked for an additional grant to complete the basement and second storey of what Bertram claimed was an unnecessarily large building. Defending their request on the grounds that Berlin, only two miles away, had received several additional grants, Waterloo was disappointed when Bertram not only refused them but pointed out that "the adoption of an injured tone in your correspondence will not alter facts."[41]

Bertram's personal association through his wife's family with Seaforth and Huron County seems to have been identified by only two communities. A letter from James Baxter of St. Marys in April 1904 congratulated Bertram on his choice of a "life partner."[42] And the President of the Clinton Board of Trade, John Ransford, used an early friendship with Mrs. Bertram to seek assistance for that community:

> I was delighted to find in Mrs. J. F. MacLaren an old friend of mine, and was still further pleased to hear from her of her sister, now Mrs. Bertram, whom I remember very well as a school girl to whom I used sometimes to give a ride, during the year that my business took me to Seaforth. I don't suppose she remembers me very well; but I would desire to be kindly remembered to her.[43]

Whether it was this childhood association that influenced Bertram or not, he did agree to provide Clinton with funds to construct a Carnegie addition to their existing library, a unique situation in this province.

At the beginning of the 20th century public libraries in Ontario were the responsibility of the Department of Education working through the Inspector of Public Libraries. During the era of Carnegie grants there were three Inspectors who became involved with various aspects of the building programme: T.W.H. Leavitt, 1905-1908, Walter R. Nursey, 1909-1915, and W.O. Carson, 1916-1929. Leavitt reported on the province's growing number of Carnegie libraries in his 1906 report:

> The establishment of Carnegie Public Libraries in some of the cities and towns of the Province has proved not only beneficial to the localities in which they have been opened, but their influence is felt in other centres of population and in rural libraries of the smallest class.
>
> In more than one locality the Carnegie Public Library is gradually becoming the natural local centre of the community. Citizens are proud of the building and its surroundings. They know that the days of doubt have passed: financially it is on a firm foundation. It rapidly makes for itself a place in the affections of the community and becomes the centre of various local interests; as the fountain of intellectual life and the agent of common culture it fills many wants felt by old and young, gradually its power for good is recognized and citizens willingly co-operate in its improvement. The personality of the librarian becomes an effective influence in the community. He ceases to be considered a watchdog to keep the people away from the books that they may be as little worn as possible, and his advice is more and more sought by the inexperienced.[44]

The report also contained a section that clearly indicated the importance placed upon the Carnegie building grant programme:

> For the assistance of Library Boards contemplating the erection of new libraries the accompaying half-tone illustrations, floor plans

and descriptions have been prepared showing some of the modern Public Libraries of the Province. The list is not complete, owing to the difficulties experienced in securing photographs and blue prints.[45]

Plans and descriptions of twenty-two libraries were included with the 1906 report, all but two of which—London and Hamilton—were Carnegie buildings as shown in Table 9.

The 1907 Report announced that a special library on building construction had been assembled in the Department of Education:

> The library on construction consists of the latest publications in the United States devoted to library building and equipment. The works include views and plans of most of the Carnegie library buildings. The plans are of exceptional value, having been supplied by the architects who designed the buildings. Illustrated publications and catalogues furnish hints as to equipment, including stacks, tables, modes of lighting, chairs, systems of heating, etc.[47]

There is no question that this special collection was frequently used by the Ontario Library Boards struggling to plan for their Carnegie libraries. Lantern slides of these same plans and photographs were also made available, either through the Department or the Ontario Library Association (O.L.A.) as was mentioned in a February, 1910 letter from Oshawa Board member S.K. Murton to his opposite number, E.M. Goodman in New Liskeard:

> . . . If you wish to secure proper information and obtain pictures of other Library buildings better apply to E. A. Hardy, Secretary, Ontario Library Association, or to W. R. Nursey, Inspector of Public Libraries. Our Board supplied photographs of interiors and exterior of our building to both these gentlemen and I think they would put you in the way of having a government official show lantern slide views of these and other buildings in your Town at a convenient date. . . . the Department has a good collection of the best Public Library buildings in Ontario, and also some American buildings, so that enquiring of the Inspector or Mr. Hardy will obtain for you full information including perhaps copies of Plans, in some cases, and figures of total cost.[48]

The Town of Orillia also took advantage of the assistance offered by the Department of Education, for in March, 1910, Mayor M. Goffatt wrote to Bertram as follows:

> The Library Board has been favoured by the Ontario Government, and have had the privilege of looking over a large number of the best ideas in library construction by way of limelight view, kindly loaned by the Government. After looking them all over and thoroughly considering everything, the Committee are meeting on the 31st inst., to see if it is possible to embody any new feature presented, other than we have already decided on in the plans as now prepared by the Architect.[49]

A letter a few weeks later referred to the fact that the Orillia Board had inspected about one hundred of the Ontario Government plans, as well as having incorporated the best ideas in Carnegie libraries in many other places.[50] The Reeve of Elora, A.J. Kerr, also referred to the "Ontario

Table 9   List of plans and descriptions[46]

Brantford	Goderich	Ottawa	St. Thomas
Brockville	Galt	Paris	Stratford
Berlin	Guelph	St. Catharines	Waterloo
Chatham	Hamilton	Sarnia	Windsor
Collingwood	Lindsay	Smiths Falls	
Cornwall	London	St. Marys	

Fergus Carnegie library. *The Fergus building was highly praised by Bertram, and its plans were made available in pamphlet form from the Department of Education.*

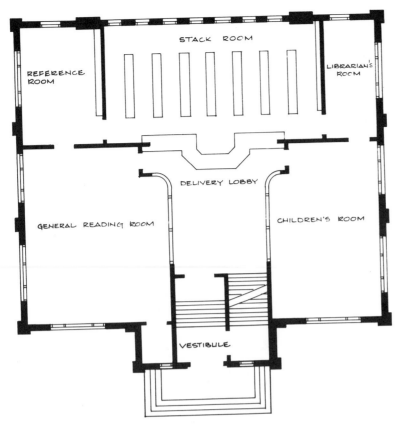

Waterloo Carnegie library, first floor plan. *The Waterloo plans were in the collection maintained by the Public Library Inspector for the use of communities planning a Carnegie building. Although the Orangeville Library Board visited Toronto in order to inspect the various plans they obviously were not able to use any because of the nature of their site.*

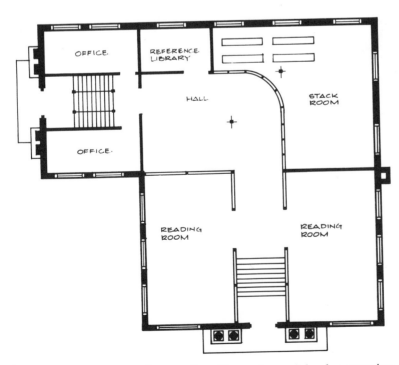

Orangeville Carnegie library, first floor plan. *A bank occupying the corner of their site made it necessary for the Orangeville building to be built around it with two main entrances.*

Government descriptions and plans of every Library Building put up in this Province" in a March, 1909 letter to Bertram.[51] The Orangeville Board travelled to Toronto to meet with Inspector Leavitt and to inspect the collection of plans in May, 1906.[52] The Town of Thorold assured Bertram that they had solicited plans from the Department of Education as well as from many Ontario towns prior to approving the sketches proposed by their architect.[53]

The collection of plans and slides assembled by O.L.A. Secretary Hardy was also used to assist in preparing plans. The communities of Picton and Brampton both mentioned that they used this material,[54] and Hardy visited Brampton personally to provide assistance.[55]

In his 1908 report, Inspector Leavitt summarized his view of library affairs in Ontario, noting the responsibilities and additional duties which expansion of the public library system was bringing to the Education Department, the Ontario Library Association, librarians and Library Boards. He thought it fortunate that "the erection of numerous library buildings through the generosity of Mr. Carnegie, has resulted in awakening of librarians and their co-workers to a realization of their responsibilities and a desire to place this Province in the foremost rank in library work.[56] A year later Inspector Nursey continued this assessment of the library scene, included more views and plans of libraries, and commented that his duties included frequent exhibition of slides of the established libraries suitable for rural communities.[57] A more direct involvement with the Carnegie building programme began that same year, as he outlined in his 1910 report:

> An interesting correspondence has taken place during the year with Mr. James Bertram, Private Secretary to Mr. Andrew Carnegie, in reference to building plans submitted to him by many Library boards in Ontario, making application for a donation from Mr. Carnegie, and which in many instances were found to be totally unsuitable, either too ornate, badly designed, or wasteful in respect to space. Mr. Bertram suggested that it might be well if the plans of all proposed library buildings be first submitted to the Department of Education for the information and general approval of the Minister. In the Regulations about to be issued will be found a rule embodying the principle laid down in Mr. Bertram's suggestion. This rule calls for the filing of all such plans with the Department, prior to erection of a library building, not for professional criticism or endorsement, but with the object of giving the board interested the benefit of the information in possession of the Department. These plans will be open for inspection by all interested. In the case of the plans of the new library at Fergus, they met with Mr. Bertram's warm approval. It is understood that Mr Carnegie is desirous that some general uniform style of architecture should be followed both in respect to exterior and interior plans of those library buildings towards the construction of which he has contributed. The Fergus building is commended on the grounds of economy of space construction and simplicity of design. The plans are reproduced elsewhere. To meet the needs of enquirers, these plans have been issued by the Department in pamphlet form. One important feature, however, appears to have been overlooked, viz.: space for a Children's department.
> With the plans of Andrew Carnegie and other architects available there is now no excuse for Library Boards to spend money in perpetuating mistakes that have been discovered and remedied.[58]

This increased involvement with the plans for the Carnegie buildings

Markdale Carnegie library. *Inspector Walter R. Nursey attended many Carnegie library openings, including that in Markdale in 1915.*

meant that approval for individual plans was frequently sought from Nursey prior to their submission either to Bertram or Franks. For example, Campbellford tried to resolve difficulties which they were having, and architect W.A. Mahoney assured Franks that: "Mr. Nursey, Public Library Inspector, has seen the plans and has approved them, and wrote me a very nice letter in regard to them."[59] Similarly Mayor E.F. Seagram of Waterloo, in attempting to persuade Bertram that a further $2,000 grant would be appropriate, wrote in 1907: "The Waterloo Carnegie Library has been most favourably commented upon by the Inspector of Libraries for the Province of Ontario, having been pronouced by him as the second best building in the Province for the money expended."[60]

Among the more pleasant duties of the Inspectors was their expected attendance at the official openings of the Carnegie buildings. *The Standard* described Markdale's Library opening on June 24, 1915 as a brilliant occasion, mentioning that Walter H. [sic] Nursey, Provincial Library Inspector, "added honour and dignity with his presence, and gave an interesting address that was highly complimentary to the book-loving intelligence of the Province." Nursey's speech was a small part of the programme. He was preceded by a voice solo by Miss Mabel Plewes which was "sung with excellent effect;" an address by Reeve Ennis of the County Council in Owen Sound which was "good and to the point;" a violin solo on "the divine instrument" by Bert Mathews; a short address of "real worth" by Dr. Sproule: a Scotch solo by Miss Jean Baird which "delighted the audience;" "a much appreciated address" by Rev. W.W. Wallace, and a "patriotic solo" by Mrs. A.M. Brown. After Nursey's presentation the evening concluded with another solo, this time by Mrs. H. Armstrong, and a "charming rendition" of Rudyard Kipling's 'Builder,' by Mrs. Scott Hall. 'God Save our King' closed a "really high class program and a most delightful evening."[61]

Inspector Carson also attended many openings, including that at Norwood on February 18, 1924. Writing to Bertram two days later, Library Board Treasurer John E. Roxburgh mentioned that Carson had "come down from Toronto to take part. From conversations with him I feel he is very much pleased with the building and also with the way the people are supporting the Board."[62]

The Department of Education and its Inspectors were frequently called upon to resolve problems or unpleasantries with the Ontario libraries which Bertram, because of distance or his lack of familiarity with Ontario legislation, could not. Inspector Nursey found it necessary to define the extent of this involvement with Carnegie Corporation affairs, and wrote to Bertram in March, 1914, stating that the Department could not "be recognized as an intermediary or special pleader for any municipality." He assured Bertram, however, that he would continue to assist him in every way possible in his dealings with the Ontario libraries.[63] Typical of the situations in which Bertram had to ask for such assistance was that which arose both in Renfrew and Welland in 1915. Neither community had passed the necessary bylaw authorizing their municipalities to levy taxes for library maintenance. Nursey investigated both towns, reporting to Bertram that in Renfrew the bylaw had passed in May, 1915 but in Welland the rate-payers had rejected it owing to lack of "correct information."[64] Similarly, Nursey informed Bertram that Tavistock was not qualified to rank as a Free Library in March, 1915 but wrote in June that a vote had been taken and the necessary bylaw had been passed by a large majority of rate-payers. Tavistock Village Clerk J.G. Field assured Bertram in July of that same year that Nursey had approved their floor plans, and that they were ready to begin construction as soon as they had a satisfactory reply from the Carnegie Corporation.[65]

It was W. O. Carson, Inspector of Public Libraries after 1916, who was involved with the final Carnegie libraries in the province. Promises of building grants had been made to seven communities between 1913-1916. In Ontario this included Stouffville and Welland, 1913, Glencoe and Norwood, 1914, Clinton and Renfrew, 1915, and Merritton, 1916. In addition, Gravenhurst had had its initial 1906 promise revived in 1916. Although efforts were made to complete some of these libraries before 1920 none of the communities had succeeded in satisfying all the conditions, and letters sent by Bertram from the Carnegie Corporation to each community in October, 1921, were similar to the one sent to Gravenhurst:

> As it is manifestly not desirable that promises of this description should remain in force indefinitely, I am directed to ascertain from you whether construction is about to be undertaken.[66]

Gravenhurst did attempt to complete their building but had difficulty getting their plans approved: the $7,000 grant would no longer provide a building that either the Library Board or Town Council wanted. Bertram refused to raise the grant, directing them to use standard Plan E or F (from "Notes on Library Bildings") as being the most practical under the circumstances. In May, 1922, he again drew their attention to "the long time this opportunity has been before your community and to the fact that it cannot be allowed to remain on the books of the Corporation indefinitely. Effective action should be taken during the present building season."[67]

Similar problems developed at Glencoe and Norwood and Inspector Carson intervened, suggesting that they adopt the same plan in order to save architect's fees, even offering to have the plans prepared in Toronto. These two libraries, like Gravenhurst, have floor plans modelled on Plan F from "Notes on Library Buildings," with very simple and unadorned exteriors. Clinton, which received money for an addition designed to match the original library, and Merritton, Renfrew and Stouffville, with larger grants, were able to build more traditional Carnegie libraries with centre entrance and portico. The Stouffville building, on the advice of Carson, is copied from Renfrew but on a smaller scale, with the architect's fee saved through the kind offices of a Department of Education architect.[68]

Welland also had difficulty in completing acceptable plans in time to secure the grant, and Mayor James Hughes had the distinction of receiving a critical letter from the Carnegie Corporation Assistant President, W.S. Learned, rather than from Bertram:

> Permit me, in the absence of the Secretary, Mr. Bertram, to acknowledge your letter of June 26 [1922] enclosing a plan for your proposed library.
>
> I judge from his drawing that the architect paid no attention to the "Notes on Erection of Library Buildings" which was sent you. The suggestions therein contained are the accumulation of many years of experience with hundreds of libraries of all sizes and should be carefully studied. Departures from these arrangements may prove desirable or permissable in the case of Welland, but in each instance such changes should be fully discussed and any reasons for them understood. Let us suggest that your architect begin again with this memorandum before him.[69]

Glencoe Carnegie library. *Glencoe was one of the last Carnegie libraries to be built in the province, opening on February 1, 1923.*

Clinton Carnegie library. *Clinton is the only Ontario Carnegie library which was actually an addition to an existing building. The Carnegie funded structure is on the right.*

Changes were made hastily and Welland was able to receive approval for their plans. However, without Inspector Carson, who kept in touch with both the libraries and with the Carnegie Corporation, Welland and the other six communities might not have been beneficiaries of these final Carnegie library building grants.

Toronto and its branches

The first letter written to Andrew Carnegie on behalf of the City of Toronto appears to have been from one of the city's best known residents, author, journalist and intellectual Goldwin Smith, on November 28, 1901. He not only asked for a grant for a building but promised to bequeath his own extensive personal collection of books to the library and to do everything he could "in making your creation worthy of your name." Since this private letter received no response, a grant was sought in June, 1902, by Toronto Board member W.F.J. Lee. Once more there was no response. Finally, in December, 1902, Chief Librarian James Bain made yet another attempt to reach Carnegie. It was to this last letter that James Bertram replied favourably and, in January, 1903, offered Toronto $350,000, if it would be used for "very fine branch libraries in addition to a Central Library." Bain negotiated successfully for three branch libraries to cost $25,000 each with the balance reserved for the central building, and the "letter of promise" was received on January 23, 1903.[1]

Interestingly, this gift, which had to be made public since it required the normal City Council approval, was not received with unanimous enthusiasm by the citizens of Toronto. Organized labour was particularly distressed, and the Toronto District Labour Council and the Council of the Allied Printing Trades both passed motions opposing the grant.[2] Others suggested that it would be "humiliating for a large city of wealth and refinement to be placed in the position of begging for a share of the Steel King's millions."[3] City Council had no such concerns, however, and they informally moved acceptance and a support pledge within a month of Bertram's promise.[4]

As in so many other communities, the choice of a library site was not straightforward, and it was not until December, 1904, that the Library Board's selection of the north-west corner of College and St. George streets was ratified by City Council. The formal resolution pledge was finally sent to Franks on May 17, 1905.[5] Having obtained the necessary approvals from the City, the Toronto Board held a competition, to close in January, 1906, in order to select an architect for the new "Reference Library." A prize of $750 was to be divided among the first three selections. After considerable deliberation the Committee of Judges (Mayor, City Councillor, Public Library Trustee, Chief Librarian, City Architect and one non-competing architect) reported in March, 1906, that no submission met the competition conditions and "recommended that no prize be awarded." Instead, $1,000 was divided among the four competitors whose plans were judged most satisfactory, and they were asked to modify their plans "in accordance with certain specified conditions."[6]

Of the modified plans the Committee chose those prepared by Wickson & Gregg and A. H. Chapman, Associated Architects, and they were awarded the contract for the Library in the summer of 1906.[7] It is interesting to note that Chapman had apprenticed with Beaumont Jarvis of Toronto, architect for Carnegie libraries in Orangeville and Lucknow, prior to attending the Ecole des Beaux Arts in Paris.[8] Chapman later designed the Carnegie libraries in Dundas and Barrie as well as the Dovercourt Branch of the Toronto Library system. Wickson & Gregg designed the Brampton Carnegie Library in 1906.

The proposed Toronto Reference Library was described in glowing terms in the 1906 Report of the Inspector of Public Libraries. Included in its outstanding features were to be a large reference room devoted entirely to readers, a circulating library of 10,000 volumes, a special reading area for teachers, and children, a five-storey "stack-house" of iron and glass construction, and exhibition space for "rare maps and local pictures."[9]

As noted above, the Toronto grant had included funds for three branch libraries. In March, 1909, the Treasurer for the Toronto Library Board, A.E. Huestis, wrote to Bertram of certain difficulties:

> We have already completed two branches at $25,000 each, and the main reference building is approaching completion. We hope to be in about the 1st of May. Now we have already moved the College St. branch into the Main Reference Building, which is located on College St. I am writing to ask if we may have your permission to call the College St. branch one of the three branches at first contemplated, and to use a portion of the $25,000 appropriated for this branch for *absolutely necessary extensions* and *alterations* to the Main Reference Building, made necessary by putting the branch in this main building.
>
> Your permission to alter the original terms of Mr. Carnegie's grant as I have suggested will help us out of a very great difficulty and enable us to complete our main Reference Building to our satisfaction, and make it by all odds the best in the Dominion.[10]

Bertram would not be fooled that a circulating library included in the original plans for the Reference Library could now be called a branch library, and informed Huestis that:

> You seem to think that money for a Branch Library and for a central Library is interchangeable. It is not. Mr. Carnegie considers the sum he provided for a Central Building ample, and if the Branch Library askt for is not required in the district and at the location decided upon, so much less should be required from Mr. Carnegie.[11]

The Board proceeded with the separate branch libraries as originally planned, so that the first three Toronto Carnegie branches were built, as Bertram had suggested, for approximately $25,000 each: Yorkville, opened in 1907; Queen and Lisgar, 1909; and Riverdale, 1910. In addition, the Carnegie Library in the community then known as Toronto Junction (later West Toronto) was renamed the Western Branch when that community was annexed by Toronto in 1909. Situated at the corner of Annette and Medland Streets, this branch is now called Annette.[12]

Grants for two additional branches had also been promised to Toronto in 1908. Remarkably, Chief Librarian George Locke was unaware of this as he explained to Bertram in a June, 1914 letter:

> In a conference with Mr. W.R. Nursey the point was raised . . . that there was an amount of $50,000 standing to the credit of the Public Library Board of Toronto according to the correspondence pass-

Toronto Reference library. *A 1903 Carnegie grant of $350,000 provided Toronto with the Reference Library (at College and St. George) and three branches: Yorkville, Riverdale, and Queen and Lisgar.*

Toronto Junction Carnegie library (now Annette branch). *Toronto Junction received a Carnegie grant in 1908, but the library was named the Western Branch when the community was annexed by Toronto in 1909. It is now called the Annette Branch.*

Wychwood Branch, Toronto Public library. *Wychwood was one of three branches built in 1915/16, with a second Carnegie grant to the City of Toronto. The recent addition (foreground) is part of the Toronto renovation programme.*

Wychwood interior showing the shelving under the windows and the reading room space with its fireplace.

ing between your office and his. It was found that this supplementary grant had been made before my appointment and while the late Mr. C. Egerton Ryerson was secretary of the Board. The untimely death of both Dr. Bain and Mr. Ryerson had caused this to be overlooked.[13]

Locke went on to describe the great expansion occurring in Toronto and the provincial statute which compelled City Council to set aside support for public libraries.

> There is a fairly complete working plan for anticipation of the city's growth so that the educational facilities of the public libraries will be within reach of all our citizens. May I say that the sketch accompanying this letter has been made to bring to the minds of the people of the outlying districts some recollections of their Scottish and English village type of architecture. These Suburbs are largely working classes from the countries mentioned.[14]

Bertram did not take kindly to the suggestion that Carnegie funds had been waiting for Toronto to use them, "Inasmuch as the promis of $50,000 for this purpos (i.e. branch libraries) has been neglected for over six years, we certainly shud have renewed application rather than the assumption that the mony, as you express it, is 'standing to your credit.' "[15]

Further complications arose because Locke and the Library Board insisted that the sites for the proposed branches be deeded to them and not held by the City Council. Bertram favoured city ownership, explaining his views quite directly:

> Our usual rule is to have title to the library site vested in the community, i.e., the city, for account of the library. If the deed specifies that the site is for library purposes there is no danger of anything going wrong. We are averse to Mayors and City Councils being kept out of library matters as if they were not to be trusted.[16]

The matter was resolved when Bertram accepted the Toronto Library Board's position, although he noted that the pledge was not strictly to the explicit wording of the Carnegie Corporation Board's standard. In any case, funds for Wychwood, High Park, and Beaches were approved in September, 1915.

The Toronto Library Board, having been so remiss in earlier years, kept the Carnegie Corporation well informed of their progress in erecting these three branches, with the Secretary-Treasurer E.S. Cogswell sending monthly reports. In November, 1915, he noted that the cornerstones had been laid for both the High Park and Beaches Branches on the same afternoon, while the Wychwood Branch was well on its way to completion. He also explained how efficiently the construction was being supervised, something which must surely have pleased Bertram. "Our own Engineer, a very capable man" Cogswell noted, "is acting as inspector on all three buildings, and keeping a very close watch. We purchased an automobile for him so that he could cover the distance between the different buildings with no unnecessary loss of time."[17]

When Bertram had written his 'promis' letter for the three branches he had included his usual request for photographs, plans and elevations of the completed buildings. A year later Bertram wrote again to Locke, noting that no pictures or report had as yet been received. George Locke's reply, September 14, 1916, is one of the more emotional letters in the Canadian Carnegie Library Correspondence:

May I draw your attention to the fact that we are handicapped by the fact that we are at war; that we have enlisted 350,000 men to defend the Mother Country; that an enlistment of that number of men severely cripples industry and other building operations in our Country. Perhaps I can put it more graphically to you when I say that if the United States mobilised five million men and sent them Abroad it would be just the same proportion as we are doing in this Country. I need not say to you that we have made every effort to complete the buildings in as short a time as possible, and I think when you see the plans of the pictures you will agree that we have spent every cent of the money in a very economical and efficient manner. I have been more careful of your money than if it were my own, and I do hope that some day some member of your Corporation will come to Toronto and see the result of your liberality.[18]

There is no record of Bertram's response. Further Carnegie grants were sought by Toronto for additional branches, for extension to the Reference Library, and to provide more space for boys and girls. None of these requests was successful.

Interior of Waterloo Carnegie library. *The circulation desk created a barrier separating the user from the bookstacks, and separate reading rooms were provided on either side of the circulation area for men and women.*

Chapter Three

"Effective Accommodation"

Plans and sites

Architectural planning is the proper arrangement of the needs and purposes of a building. Although planning for the Carnegie libraries was obviously considered by Bertram to be the most important factor in the building project, he refrained from giving advice about the development of the plans. Initially he left the planning process entirely up to the community, its Library Board and its architect, only interfering when plans were brought to his attention through, for example, requests for an additional grant.

George Locke, Chief Librarian of Toronto from 1908, had differing and very strong views about the limitations of leaving library planning to architects or elected officials, as opposed to those who would work in the buildings:

> No Library ought to be planned for any size of a community without the aid of a librarian who has had experience in library planning. He is just as useful to the community which hopes to build as is an architect, because he can appreciate the problem from a professional point of view and can see the necessities from the social and practical point of view of the community to be served. Then comes the architect to whom the problem is now put in plain understandable terms, and he is asked to make the proportionate spaces and house in the plan in such a way that the exterior will be attractive and the inside economically efficient, and with such building materials and finish as will make for comfort, attractiveness and a minimum of expenditure for maintenance.
>
> One cannot expect Library Boards to know what is wanted. They are made up of men from as many vocations in life as there are members, and the bad examples of library construction are due almost entirely to a Board commissioning a local architect to build a library to cost say $15,000, without any thought of asking the Inspector of Public Libraries or any of the active librarians of the province to give them any advice. It is a clear case too often of the blind teaching the blind—and the monument to their folly can be seen in too many of our towns.[1]

Few libraries had someone as informed or as respected as George Locke on hand, and it was not until the Carnegie grant programme was well underway that Bertram realized that changes had to be made. Problems with the plans became evident when, as noted, a building could not be constructed within the original amount granted. When the community then asked for an additional grant, as they did almost without exception, Bertram insisted on seeing the plans. By 1907 he had seen so many poor and inadequate plans that from that date on he insisted on plan approval prior to awarding the grant. The Brussels Library Board, for example, received the following post-script to the standard "promise" letter of February 6, 1907:

> P.S. Should like to see plans of proposed building before you commit yourselves to any expenditure. Altho Mr. Carnegie does not object to a small auditorium or lecture room, that feature must not over shadow that of the Library proper.[2]

Upon receiving plans which he felt were unsuitable, it was not unusual for Bertram to send them to New York architects with library experience for specific criticisms[3] which he then relayed to the community. After considerable discussion of several plans submitted by Grand Valley beginning in 1909, the following detailed critique was received from Bertram in May, 1911:

> As you are apparently wedded to a bilding covering an area of 38×52 ft., I submitted your plans to an architect expert in Library planning and find that from an architectural point of view the following criticisms are to be made on your plans.
> The bilding has an unnecessarily high roof; it is insufficiently lited; the construction is improper, the colums, in some cases not resting on supports below. This is in addition to what I have alredy pointed out to you that the depth of the bilding results in a long passage and uneconomical arrangement.[4]

A sketch was included which he recommended as being more appropriate, but apparently Grand Valley and their architect did not agree. Bertram sent the following letter to Reeve James Reith a few weeks later, expressing his frustration with the whole procedure as well as his philosophy of library buildings and floor layouts:

> You must be aware that while preserving an appearance of taking advice, you are requesting all. We have written and receivd a score of letters in connection with these Grand Valley plans and hav not progress at all, becaus you adhere to your own set ideas in spite of experienced advice. The burden of your last letter is that you like the appearance of the accommodation better in your plans, whereas, the object ought to be economical arrangement and affectiv working.
> When you write, pleas return the sketch plan sent you and at the same time giv your practical reasons for not adopting same, apart from what you call 'appearance.' What is wanted in a small bilding like this is the maximum of effectiv accommodation, not to aim at an appearance of dignity and importance.[5]

Although this issue of "effective accommodation" was to him most important, there were other details of design and layout which Bertram frequently criticized and about which he also made positive recommendations. Thorold, for example, was told that there was no necessity for a second storey and, further, a staff entrance was uncalled for in a $10,000 building.[6] Board Rooms as well were deemed unnecessary. Bertram explained to the Secretary of the Harriston Board, A.G. Campbell, that "the infrequent meetings of the Board can be held in the Librarians' room, the reference library, or, in fact, anywhere rather than to take up valuable accommodations for the purpose."[7]

Forest, on submitting two sets of plans, had one set returned because they contained a "useless rotunda," with the entrance steps on the inside rather than outside as Bertram preferred. Bertram also criticized placing reading rooms out of sight of the librarian's supervision, and he disliked permanent partitions, recommending instead that all library functions be placed on one floor with books shelved around the room. Any necessary partitions could be, he argued, formed of moveable bookcases adjusted to meet changing needs.[8]

Toronto's Locke similarly favoured simple one-room libraries, which would allow the main function—the intermingling of books and people— to occur, unimpeded. "Take away all unnecessary decorations, over-mantels, over-counters, partitions, mock marble pillars and large hall-ways," he urged, "and plan a well proportioned room with books on the walls, small and few tables, a simple charging desk (not a great counter), simple lighting as near the books and the people as possible, and a combination of colours in the walls that make for harmony." He concluded: "Then take away all 'Silence' signs and let the people come and talk about the books in an atmosphere of social happiness."[9] The floor plan of the Wychwood Branch illustrates this simplicity.

A staircase at one end of the room leading to the lecture hall below and the fireplace at the other are all that intruded on a symmetrical layout of wall shelving, with large and small reading tables arranged as needs dictated. The other two later Toronto Carnegie Branches, Beaches and High Park, had identical layouts.

While Toronto may have accepted the concept of wall shelving, most Library Boards preferred a stack room which, if not actually closed at all times, certainly could be. Bertram debated this issue with the Secretary of the Shelburne Library Board, T.F.E. Claridge in 1911, pointing out that:

> The books can be arranged around the walls of the bilding and you hav to consider whether it would not be advisable to make your bilding a regular block insted of having the part jutting out behind. This would allow of the main block being enlarged somewhat and by saving the flite of steps (inside the stack room) you could bring the delivery desk forward nearer the door and let the Librarian sit in the center of what would be practically one large room from which all parts of it could be supervised.[10]

Claridge responded that visits had been made to several neighbouring Carnegie libraries and, in talking to librarians, he had concluded that the Shelburne plans, including a stack room, had been found more favourable. His argument was persuasive:

> We are very sorry indeed to hear your objections to a stack room. Personally I have had experience with both systems in our own library here, and I would say by all means have your stack room separate if possible no matter how small your library. When books, reading tables and all were in one room it did not prove satisfactory for us, for we found the movements of the librarian were always an interruption and annoyance to the readers, while at the same time the librarian

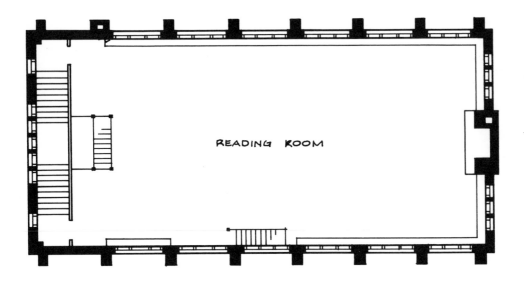

Wychwood Branch library, first floor plan. *These floor plans, with book shelves around the walls, were considered by Bertram to be the best arrangement for "effective accommodation."*

Table 10   Corner buildings

Guelph 1901
Brockville 1903
Dundas 1904
Perth 1906
Brussels 1909
Toronto: Riverdale Branch 1909

was put to constant annoyance by the readers having too free access to the books and being entirely care free as to where or how they put them back on the shelves.[11]

Bertram subsequently compromised on this point, allowing Shelburne its stack room and concentrating his objections on the unnecessary stairway and Board Room. The stairway was eliminated and the Board Room was combined with the Librarian's office before Bertram gave his final approval and authorized Franks to begin payment for the building.

Ceiling heights also concerned Bertram. Barrie was told that "we do not consider that a $15,000 library bilding needs a ceiling 15 ft. in the clear. The ceiling can be a least 3 ft. lower and still be ample for all practical purposes." Barrie architect A.H. Chapman disagreed, replying that lowering the ceiling would save little in the total costs and would "detract considerably from the proportion of the exterior." Nevertheless the Barrie plans were changed before final approval was received.[12]

Among the plans which Bertram disliked most were those for a corner library, although he admitted that for some sites this would be necessary and included a sample in his 1911 instructional booklet, "Notes on Library Bildings." Hespeler was informed that "the adoption of a corner entrance in itself entailed a sacrifice of an unusual proportion of the available area to entrance features."[13] Only the following small number of communities, however, chose sites which necessitated corner buildings, so corner siting was not a major element in the planning of the Ontario Carnegie libraries:

A rotunda or non-functional vestibule in any of the early plans was also a feature for which Bertram expressed particular disapproval. The first floor plan of Brantford was severely criticized when that city applied for a grant to extend their original library. Bertram noted that: "A rotunda is not only unnecessary . . . but besides being a most expensive feature it leads to waste of space where every dollar should tell in effectiv accommodation. In this plan the 24 feet square under the rotunda is almost all waste because there is a delivery room between it and the delivery counter."[14] This same feature in the Sarnia library was referred to as an "ambitious rotunda [which] has entirely spoiled the building."[15]

Other early floor plans, which could never have passed the close scrutiny which Bertram later imposed include Goderich, which in addition to the irregular plan form caused by its two towers had living quarters for either the librarian or caretaker on the second floor. Perth put such quarters in its basement, and at least five other libraries seem also to have planned for this function: Aylmer, Hanover, Harriston, Smiths Falls, and Stratford.

The Waterloo plans were much admired by many other libraries but were not favoured by Bertram. This was a closed stack library as were many of those built in the early years of the grant programme, although access could be permitted by the librarian if it was considered appropriate.

One of the most unusual floor plans was that in Lindsay, which received its grant in 1902. Bertram was probably unaware of the faceted semi-circular stack room since he was not reviewing floor plans at that time, but this feature, and its lack of expandability, was criticized in the 1906 Report of the Public Library Inspector.[16] A similar approach was used for the stack room in Chatham.

Having spent so much time trying to correct mistakes after they had been made, Bertram finally decided that a better approach would be to prevent blunders before they occurred. Conferences with leading au-

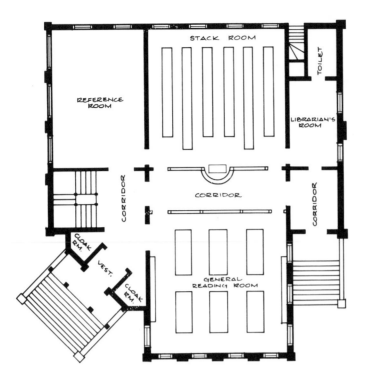

Brockville Carnegie library, first floor plan. *Brockville, a corner building,*
illustrates a floor plan which Bertram considered wasteful.

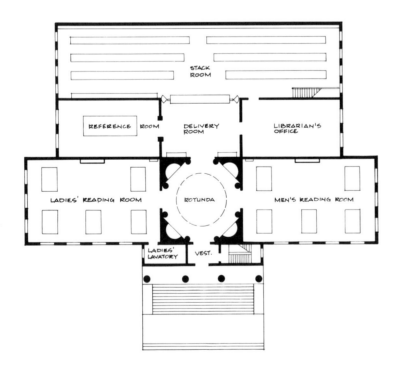

Brantford Carnegie library: first floor plan. *The earlier Carnegie libraries*
frequently had features which Bertram considered "entirely unsuited for the
purposes of a free public library." The rotundas in the Brantford and Sarnia
libraries illustrate one such feature; the triangular plan shape, cut up rooms
and the tower of the Goderich library would never have passed the inspection
which Bertram imposed after 1907.

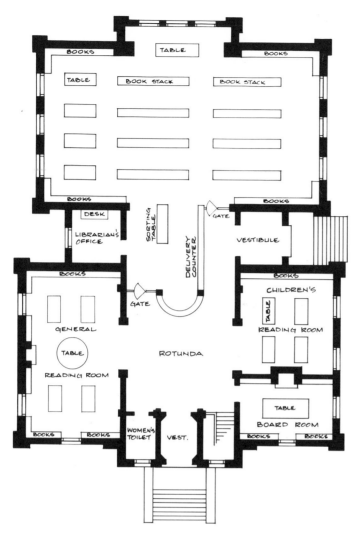

Sarnia Carnegie library: *first floor plan*.

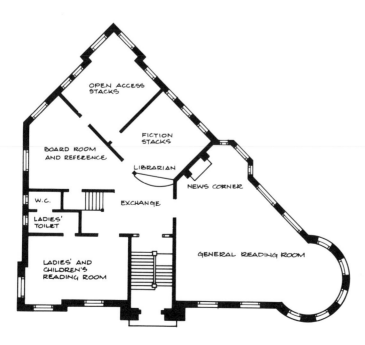

Goderich Carnegie library: *first floor plan*.

109

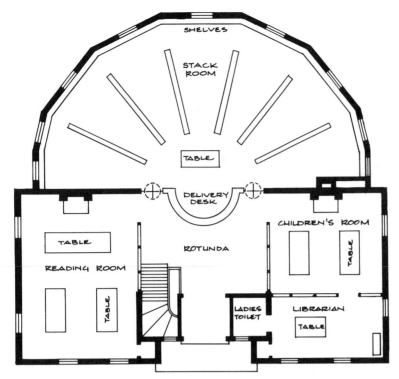

Lindsay Carnegie library: first floor plan. *Both Lindsay and Chatham were also designed with wasteful rotundas or delivery halls, but in addition had separate stack rooms which, because of their round or octagonal shapes, could not provide an efficient arrangement for bookstacks.*

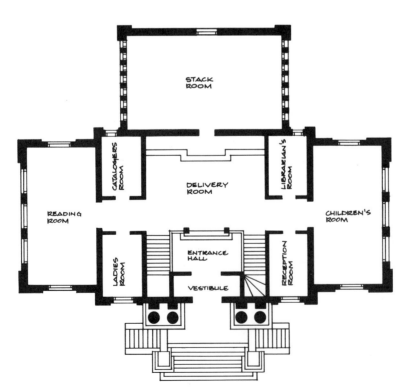

Ottawa Carnegie library: first floor plan. *This plan, called the modified 'T', was much admired by Ontario Library Boards, since it allowed the separate stack room which so many considered desirable. Bertram, however, was not enthusiastic, claiming that separate stack areas reduced flexibility and increased the number of staff members required for library operation.*

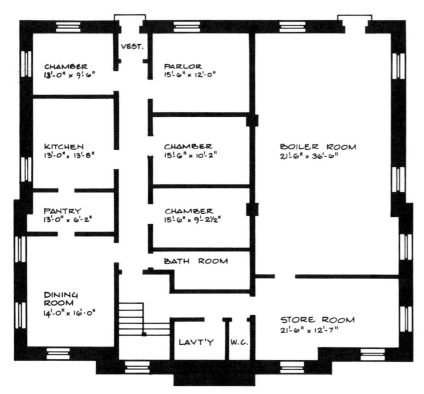

Stratford Carnegie library: basement plan. *Stratford was among the few Ontario libraries which provided living quarters for either the librarian or caretaker. Those at Stratford show an elaborate and spacious three bedroom apartment. Two of the bedrooms had no exterior windows and the Stratford Library Board attempted, without success, to persuade Bertram to fund an addition which would have rectified this deficiency.*

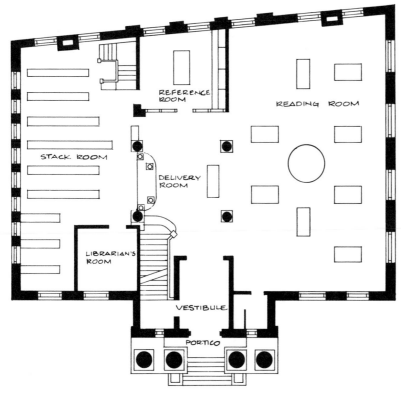

Galt Carnegie library: first floor plan. *The Galt plans are interesting because the rear wall conforms to the bank of the Grand River.*

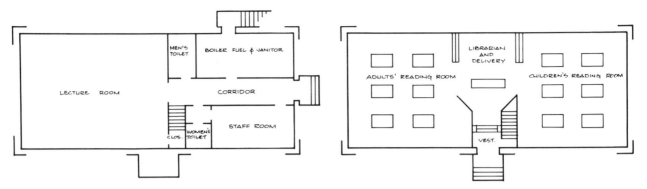

Plan A: basement.

Plan A: first floor.

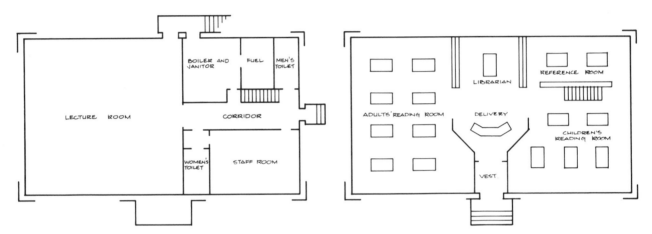

Plan B: basement.

Plan B: first floor.

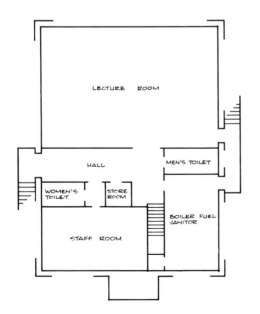

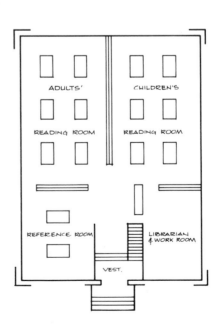

Plan C: basement.

Plan C: first floor.

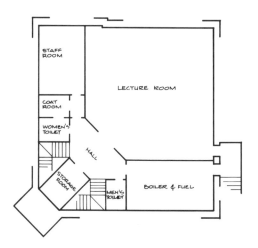
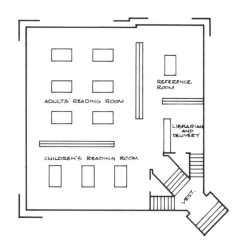

Plan D: basement.

Plan D: first floor.

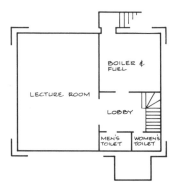
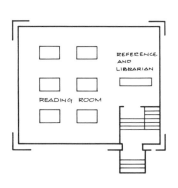

Plan E: basement.

Plan E: first floor.

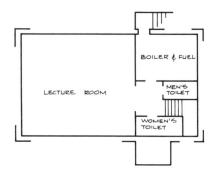
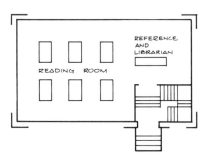

Plan F: basement.

Plan F: first floor.

Plans A-F were included in the memorandum "Notes on the Erection of Library Bildings" sent as a guide to communities planning a Carnegie library after 1911. Although the plans are for different-sized buildings — or sites — they have many features in common, most notably the accommodation of the book collection around the walls, and the use of bookstacks to create the separation of functions. The later libraries, such as Gravenhurst, were directed to use plan E or F, since the value of the grant would no longer encompass a building as large, for example, as Plan B.

thorities from the American library and architectural professions brought about agreement on certain standards in library architecture. The result was a leaflet entitled: "Notes on Library Bildings"[17] which was sent after 1911 as a guide to each community receiving the promise of funds.

There were several versions of "Notes on Library Bildings," although the differences were slight. With the text were four recommended floor plans, A to D, later expanded to include E and F. These six plans are shown below. However it was too late for "Notes on Library Bildings" to have a noticeable impact on the Ontario Carnegie libraries. Of the 111 Ontario buildings, only 39, or 35 per cent, were planned in 1911 or later.[18]

The "Notes on Library Bildings" reflected many of the comments that Bertram had directed, thus far, to various Ontario libraries, with his primary concern remaining "effective accommodation . . . consistent with good taste." To him, a "Greek temple or a modification of it" was a cause of waste.[19] Specific details which were recommended included:

- A rectangular building;
- One storey and basement, with outside staircase;
- One large room subdivided by bookcases;
- A basement four feet below grade;
- Ceiling heights of 9 feet for the basement and 12 to 15 feet for the main floor;
- Rear and side windows seven feet from floor to allow continuous wall shelving;
- A lecture room as a subordinate feature in the basement.[20]

The difference between Bertram's recommended floor plans and those of the earlier Ontario Carnegie libraries is obvious. No stack room is provided for separation of the books from the public. Neither are there any rooms except those created by book shelves or for the protection of functions such as boiler and furnace. It is also interesting to note that Bertram did not include fireplaces, a feature so favoured by Toronto and popular in most other Ontario Carnegie libraries.

Bertram entered into few theoretical discussions about the merits of "Notes on Library Bildings," with Ontario libraries. The letter from A.H. Chapman, who had been involved in the design of the Toronto Reference Library, is therefore most interesting. Having difficulty in securing acceptance for the Barrie Library plans in 1915, he had been referred by Bertram to "Notes on Library Bildings" and invited to comment. Chapman's response:

> You ask us if there are any architectural comments we would care to make upon the "Notes on the Erection of Library Bildings." There are only two points that strike us in this connection, one being a certain difficulty we have experienced in placing bookcases under the windows, as in the ordinary heating used for these buildings it is the most desirable place for the radiators. The other point is for the buildings costing over $15,000.00 a large undivided room with a comparatively low ceiling is, architecturally, not generally attractive. We can readily understand, however, the practical value and that such a recommendation saves the waste and mishandling that has so often been indulged in.[21]

No evidence suggests that Bertram thanked Chapman for his advice, but he did compromise his views and allowed the Barrie Library to proceed without strict adherence to his guidelines.

After 1911 Bertram frequently recommended a specific floor plan from "Notes on Library Bildings," and he constantly admonished Library Boards or Town Councils that their architect was not following the suggested layouts. Exeter was requested to use Plan C, while Parkhill, Stirling, Kingsville, Markdale and New Hamburg followed Plan A or B. Gravenhurst was told that plan E or F would be most suitable for them, as was Stouffville, while Hespeler was instructed to follow Plan D. Even with such specific instructions it could not be assumed that planning would proceed without difficulty. Bertram wrote to Exeter in response to a request for exact measurements that "Considering that you have our amplified 'Notes on the Erection of Library Bildings' with a diagram it should not be necessary for you to get measurements. "Your architect," he chastised, "can easily plan bilding with advantageous lay-out from the data given, if he has a mind to."[22] Bertram was undoubtedly aware that the Exeter architect, Walter Mahoney, had previously designed some nine Carnegie libraries. Financial agent Franks showed similar exasperation in a letter to Kemptville in 1911. "After receiving the 'Notes on Library Building' sent you by Mr. Bertram a few weeks ago, we are amazed at the plans for a Library Building which you submit. With perhaps one exception, in the many hundreds of library plans examined by us we have not seen plans so entirely unsuited for the purpose."[23]

It should not be assumed that all communities experienced difficulty in having their floor plans approved, athough most did. Preston and Fort Frances, which were among the later libraries, received approval with no questions or difficulties whatsoever, and only minor adjustments were required by several other communities.

Bertram, in his "Notes on Library Bildings," did not include advice to municipal Councils or Library Boards on sites suitable for the library buildings. It was assumed that the libraries would be built in downtown areas on a reasonably accessible site. In many communities, such as Waterloo and St. Marys, the library was adjacent to the town hall, reinforcing civic pride. In St. Marys, a "stone town," this pride is further emphasized by the matching of stone and ornamentation in both buildings. Brantford's library, built on the central axis of Wellington Square, shares space with the court house and is flanked by a pair of churches. A large number of the smaller town libraries are sited among the commercial or civic buildings on one of the two main streets. The Smiths Falls library is located on a treed lot at the edge of the main commercial centre, rotated on plan 45 degrees so that the main entrance is plainly visible as one walks up the street. Such prominent siting was the norm for Carnegie libraries in most Ontario communities.

Bertram did criticize a few of the building sites chosen. Grand Valley, he complained, would have to spend additional "monies" on foundations to overcome the slope of the property.[24] Both Fort William and Hespeler were criticized because their buildings occupied the entire sites; Hespeler had to change its plans in order to fit its library onto the unfortunately small site which had been chosen.[25]

Location alone was not all that interested most communities, and it was not unusual for the Horticultural Society or some other service group in the smaller towns to assume the task of maintaining the lawns and gardens around their libraries. George Locke wrote with pride about the honour accorded two of the Toronto branches in this regard. "In connection with all these Public Libraries," he explained, "there are gardens which help to make beautiful and attractive these centres of the community life, and in the case of both Wychwood and Earlscourt the silver

St. Marys Carnegie library. *The Carnegie library was located in the midst of civic buildings in most small Ontario communities. In St. Marys the library was built of like stone, with similar ornamentation.*

cups awarded by the local Horticultural Societies for the best kept and most attractive grounds in connection with public buildings in the district were won by these Libraries."[26]

Design

The first two decades of the twentieth century saw the construction of all but seven of the Ontario Carnegie libraries. As has been noted earlier, the majority of these buildings were in small communities, with populations ranging from less than 1,000 to 15,000, and with no previous separate library building. Although a building type based on academic library architecture might be considered appropriate for the larger libraries such as Toronto and Hamilton, there was no established model for most of the Ontario buildings.[1] At the same time, these new libraries did have one thing in common: they represented an important element in the civic fabric of the community.

The late nineteenth century had seen a shift, particularly in North American architecture, from the heady eclecticism of high Victorian design to a re-emergence of neo-classical taste—at least for smaller civic and commercial buildings. Through this revival of classicism ran contemporary threads of the design philosophies formulated and taught in Paris at the Ecole des Beaux-Arts. At this famous school students used systematic architectural principles and logical thought to evolve unity of design. By allowing the principal element clearly to dominate and by sacrificing the secondary elements, plans were reduced to simple functional expressions, with many details influenced by classic traditions.[2]

A steady stream of North American architects attended the Ecole during the latter part of the nineteenth century and returned, primarily to the United States, to put these principles into practice. Centres of American cities gradually filled with Beaux-Arts buildings—banks, city halls and court houses—and it was widely believed that they formally expressed strength, purpose, and above all, civic virtue through their use of traditional form and visual order.[3] By the 1880's these principles and philosophies were well established throughout the North American continent, and by the turn of the century there was no reason to doubt that a library should be included with other civic buildings as a permanent monument to learning and culture. What better way to express this belief than through the use of the accepted classical detailing of pediments and columns and the traditional orders: Doric, Ionic and Corinthian.[4]

The predominant features of many of the Ontario Carnegie library buildings have their origins in this classicism, with plans and elevations clearly revealing Beaux-Arts theories of symmetry and classical detailing. The majority of these buildings were single storey with exposed basements, and had centrally located main entrances with classically columned porticos and a symmetrical arrangement of windows.

Although this style was most popular in the smaller urban or rural communities of Ontario, it was not favoured by all. The later Toronto branches of Wychwood, Beaches and High Park, all opened in 1916, are examples of a deliberate departure from the more traditional design. George Locke wrote about his involvement in the planning and design of these buildings in the *Journal of the Royal Architectural Institute of Canada*:

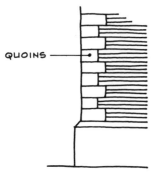

Quoins.
Units of stone or brick used to emphasize
the corners of a building.

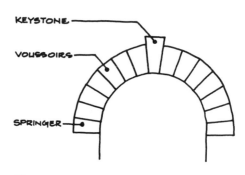

Elements of an arch.

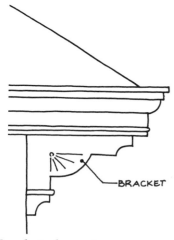

Bracketed cornice.
The support element under eaves,
cornice or other overhang,
frequently more ornamental
than functional.

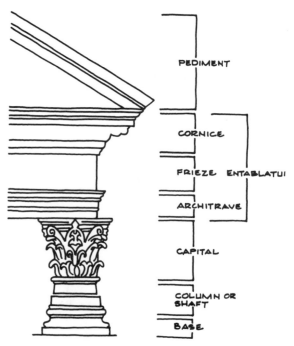

Elements of a classical portico.

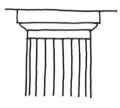  

Doric Capital.　　　　Ionic Capital.　　　　Corinthian Capital.

The top decorated element of a column or pilaster, which supports the
entablature.

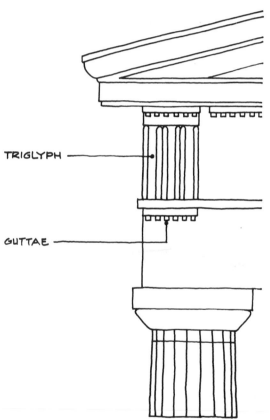

TRIGLYPH

GUTTAE

Doric order showing triglyph and
guttae in relationship to the
entablature.

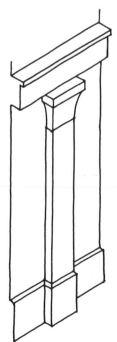

Pilaster.
A shallow pier attached to the building,
usually decorated to resemble
a classical column.

When I was planning the Wychwood Branch I was reproached by a gentleman in this city who said, 'It doesn't look like a library.' I asked him what a Library looked like. He said he didn't know but he thought it ought to have columns in front. I found out that he had seen the so-called typical Library of the Early-Carnegie days with columns in front, rooms on either hand, and a stack room in the back centre. Indeed it was an architect who told me that a Branch Library, indeed any library, should be classical in style. I couldn't find out from him whether it was Greek or Neo-Greek he favoured.[5]

Locke had described his concept of library architecture in some detail in a 1915 letter to Bertram, outlining his plans for Wychwood:

I am enclosing with this letter a description of the building, which I propose to erect. May I point out to you that it is an almost entire departure from the traditional library building, but, as I mentioned in a former letter to you, I am doing this as a result of my experience in having regard to the kinds of people who are living in this locality. These are people from the Old Country, accustomed to see in their country villages architecture of the 17th Century, and I am proposing to reproduce some of that Collegiate Grammar School architecture of the time of Edward VIth, and adapted to modern requirements. I am fortunate in having for this purpose an architect whose work is distinguished on this Continent for its adaptation of English architecture to American requirements.[6]

That architect was Eden Smith and he had his own architectural views on the chosen style. "An adaptation of English 17 Century collegiate style of architecture was chosen for this building," he said, "because the plan of its requirements and the material, brick and stone, found most convenient to use in creating it are not at all appropriate for a monumental type of building of Greek or Roman origin."[7]

The classical details and monumentalism, so deplored by Locke and Smith, can most easily be recognized in the small brick or stone library built on a raised podium, served by a single flight of exterior stairs, with columns or pilasters and variously designed capitals supporting entablatures and pediments. Brantford, representing one of the larger buildings, has an imposing projected portico with four evenly spaced columns, Ionic capitals and a plain entablature and pediment. Woodstock's portico in stone, with a lower podium than that of Brantford, has six elegantly fluted columns in two groups of three, with Corinthian capitals supporting a stone entablature and pediment.

Some architects did not give sufficient visual weight to the columns. For example, Brockville, one of the more handsome Carnegie libraries with its carefully designed entablature and portico, has its visual integrity challenged by the overly slim columns. Port Elgin, a classically symmetrical building has four undersized columns with overly large Ionic capitals, giving the building a strange loss of scale. Ayr's four portico columns, with an unusual four tiered capital and a flattened pediment over, give an unfortunate lightness to the appearance of the upper portion of the building. However, for the most part, the classical detailing was well represented. Watford's elegance and simplicity in both columns and pediment is matched in the libraries of Lindsay, St. Marys or Elmira, among many others.

The proportions of the two storey library buildings, which demanded special care in handling the design of the columns, are also

120

Beaches Branch, Toronto. *The simplicity of the Toronto Beaches Branch, designed by Toronto architect Eden Smith in what he called an English 17th century style of architecture, contrasts with the classical detailing and monumentalism of the Brantford Library.*

Brantford Carnegie library.

Column caps and pediment, Shelburne Carnegie library. *A bracketed pediment over a plain frieze supported by columns with modified Ionic capitals.*

Column capitals, Woodstock Carnegie library. *A handsome example of a Corinthian capital quite clearly illustrates the acanthus leaf design.*

Column capitals, Hamilton Carnegie library. *The neo-classical design of the Hamilton Carnegie library was reflected in the appearance of the column capitals, which combine elements of modified Ionic and Corinthian orders.*

Mount Forest Carnegie library entrance and portico. *Columns and pilasters with Ionic capitals as well as brick quoins and bracketed cornice were often included in the Ontario Carnegie library ornamentation.*

Ingersoll Carnegie library. *Ornamental keystones over main entrance and windows, combined with semi-circular bracketed pediment are some of the unusual features of the Ingersoll Carnegie library. Although not a requirement, some libraries included the name Carnegie in the building designation.*

Detail of the Ingersoll ornamentation showing an Ionic capital.

St. Catharines Carnegie library. *The owls on the pediment of the*
St. Catharines library were a distinctive feature and one of them can still
be seen in the new library.

excellent. Both Galt and Peterborough have four columns successfully grouped in pairs about the main entrance. Peterborough, with Ionic capitals and paired brackets above each capital had the distinction of curved bricks making up the round columns.

Milverton, a red brick building without a portico, has one of the most highly articulated front facades of the Ontario Carnegie libraries. Two pairs of pilasters, brick band coursing, quoins with stone band course, both sills and an archway over the main entrance with the voussoirs picked out in alternating brick and stone, gives an already busy facade a most imposing appearance. Similar detailing, although on a lesser scale, appears in other brick faced buildings such as Barrie and Stratford. Ingersoll used a bracketed cornice and massive decorated keystones to provide its ornamentation. The simplicity of design in the Weston Library is enriched by Art Nouveau mosaic panels over the windows and main entrance, a unique feature among the Ontario Carnegie libraries.

Ornamentation of the entablatures and pediments over main entrances took a number of different forms. The most commonly found items are dates and circular windows, the latter frequently framed in stone and placed in the centre of the pediment, while the dates were either painted or carved in stone. The words PUBLIC LIBRARY are found on the frieze area of some of the entablatures and the word CARNEGIE appears in a few instances (for example at Milverton, Seaforth and Ingersoll). The New Liskeard design went further in case anyone should become confused as to the function and locale of the building, by displaying clear identification and purpose with the words NEW LISKEARD PUBLIC LIBRARY in a projected stone plaque over the main entrance. The St. Catharines Carnegie building, unfortunately demolished to make way for a new court house, incorporated into the pediment a circular window with the date 1903 split up on either side of the window, and in the frieze area of the entablature the words PUBLIC LIBRARY were superimposed on a plaque complete with triglyphs and guttae. St. Catharines also added to the pediment a pair of ornamental embellishments which at first sight appeared to be urns; on closer examination they proved to be owls.

A comparison of the Carnegie libraries designed by the same architect reveals some fascinating similarities as well as idiosyncrasies in the use of the classical model. W. E. Binning, who was responsible for at least eight buildings, used three basic designs. Hanover and Harriston are similar in their Palladian plan form, and their columns have Ionic capitals with a curious double banding. (This was later repeated at Ayr giving a somewhat bizarre result.) Listowel, Binning's first library, is identical to that of Mitchell except for the exterior materials: precast stone and red brick, and the Romanesque main entrance archways with adjacent short towers provides a distinctly baronial flavour to both. Teeswater and Beaverton are almost identical, with typical entablature and pediment detailing but having unusual recessed panels rather than columns on either side of the main entrance. Preston is very similar, sharing the window arrangements including the detail of three small windows grouped over the doorway, in addition to the chimney and roof design. Preston differs from Teeswater and Beaverton in its columned portico with semi-circular pediment, an unusual feature in this province. Binning's use of the banded columns is also repeated in the Preston building.

There is another interesting relationship in Binning's work which, unfortunately, cannot be verified. The Harriston and Hanover libraries, which he designed in 1908 and 1910, bear a remarkable similarity to the

Smiths Falls Library designed in 1903 by architect G. M. Bayley of Ottawa. There is no question that Hanover was copied from Harriston. A letter from the Hanover Municipal Clerk John Taylor to Bertram in May, 1910 states: "I am sending under separate cover plans of Library Building now adopted by our Council. These plans are the same as those used by the Town of Harriston. Mr. Carnegie granted Harriston $10,000 on those plans, and Harriston, which is some 20 miles south of Hanover, has some 500 less population."[8]

The Harriston correspondence reveals that planning for that Library began in 1907. A letter from Library Board Secretary A.G. Campbell notes: "The Committee (of Board and Town Council) obtained information from 9 or 10 Towns where Carnegie Libraries are established or in course of erection, and visited five or six of them with a view to getting fullest information on the subject, and particularly as to the style of building and cost which would be most in keeping with our circumstances and requirements."[9] In July, 1908, Campbell wrote again, informing Bertram that the Board had selected as architect: "Mr. W. E. Binning who planned and supervised the erection of the Carnegie Library in Listowel. Mr. Binning is now drafting a sketch of our proposed Carnegie Library."[10] It can be suggested, therefore, with some certainty, that among the libraries visited by the Harriston Committee was that in Smiths Falls. Moreover, the floor plans and elevations of the Smiths Falls library were listed in the reports of the Inspector of Public Libraries in Toronto as being available and free for the use of Library Boards. Although Binning did not record his debt to those plans it is difficult not to believe that he was influenced to a large degree by them.

Walter Mahoney is an architect more difficult to categorize since some of the most beautiful as well as some of the strangest of the Ontario Carnegie libraries are among the fourteen which we know he designed. At Aylmer, Tillsonburg, Watford and Elmira, Mahoney used a simple classical design, while at Forest, Durham and Fergus he modified it, reducing the height of the main entrance columns and giving a heavy appearance to the upper portico. He seems to have favoured round headed windows and fanlights, repeating them in all but Stirling and possibly Campbellford (recent exterior renovations have unfortunately hidden the original design of Campbellford, and have removed the main entrance portico at Port Hope).

The influence of Mahoney's work went beyond the buildings he actually designed. As noted earlier, Bertram frequently recommended the plan for the Fergus Library, designed by Mahoney in 1908, and the Department of Education provided the floor plans to any who requested them. To architect George Gray, who designed Grand Valley, Mount Forest and Walkerton, he wrote that "the Fergus plans are probably the best that can be done with a square building . . ."[11] and Grand Valley was told that it was their departure from the Fergus plans that had resulted in Bertram's criticism. Mahoney himself admitted that he copied the Fergus plans, explaining to Bertram in the letter which accompanied the blueprints for the Durham Library, that he had "built one something like this for the Town of Fergus."[12]

Of the architects who designed two or three of the buildings, some favoured similar if not identical details while others did not. Essex and Kingsville, both designed by J. C. Pennington, are basically the same library with superficial differences. Palmerston and Guelph, designed by W. Frye Colwill, had nothing in common whatsoever. The Toronto branch libraries, although the responsibility of one Library Board, also have

Hanover Carnegie library.

Smiths Falls Carnegie library.

Harriston Carnegie library. *The Palladian character of architect G.M. Bayley's design for Smiths Falls was clearly repeated by W.E. Binning in the Harriston and Hanover designs, including such details as the graduated windows in the side pavilions.*

Watford Carnegie library. *This is one of the most attractive small Carnegie libraries in the province. Graceful paired columns with Doric capitals support a plain entablature and pediment. Simple but beautifully proportioned windows are functionally arranged and meticulously located.*

Mount Forest Carnegie library. *The two main windows are uncharacteristically small in this classical Carnegie library.*

Tavistock Carnegie library, 1916. *The standard shape of the smaller Carnegie library has been used in Tavistock, but without the more usual classical detailing common in the previous decade.*

Milverton Carnegie library. *The highly articulated front facade of the Milverton library was not repeated elsewhere in the province.*

similarities and differences. The last of these branches, Wychwood, High Park and Beaches, as noted earlier, are identical as a result of the control imposed by Locke and the work of one architect, Eden Smith. The earlier branches each had different architects and were a variation of the neo-classical idiom. Yorkville is quite similar to many of the rural Southern Ontario libraries, with two pairs of columns, projected portico, Doric capitals, a bracketed cornice, and stone quoins, band courses and key-stones. Riverdale, however, has a neo-classical corner design.

The Toronto Reference Library at College and St. George deserves particular mention, since it has a special place as the largest among the Ontario Carnegie libraries. The strong neoclassical design, influenced by A.H. Chapman's Beaux-Arts training and New York experience, is ex-pressed in the symmetrically arranged pavilions housing the College Street entrances, the reduced articulation and sober handling of windows and their adjacent panels. The College Street (front) facade, with paired ground floor windows set in a smooth grey stone wall, contrasts with the six bays above, defined by the brick pilasters and modified Corinthian capitals. The bracketed cornice and rounded pediments facing College Street give way to a plainer facade on St. George Street, with the subtle change in window proportions reflecting changed interior functions.

The library built with the smallest Ontario Carnegie grant, Kempt-ville, should also be described. The grant was only $3000 and the building was not completed until 1912. This small precast stone library, although clearly inexpensive, did manage to have a modest portico, columns and pilasters. There is no superfluous decoration but the library's function is perfectly, albeit modestly, expressed.

The later Ontario Carnegie libraries do not fall into the category of Beaux-Arts inspired designs. Norwood, Gravenhurst, Stouffville and Glencoe, having been delayed by problems in securing their grants and by the first world war, economized by sharing the same asymmetrical plan, Plan F, from "Notes on Library Bildings." No classical embellish-ments can be seen and only the typical basement and first floor arrange-ment of windows hint at the function which the buildings fulfill. Bertram described the style of architecture suitable for these small libraries as "cottage", recommending "a gable end over the door" as the only dis-tinguishing feature in a letter to Inspector Carson in 1922.[13]

Clinton, an existing two storey library building with a tower and round headed windows, was the only library to be given a grant for an extension to a non-Carnegie library. This extension repeated some of the details of the original building. Simcoe, somewhat similar to the "gram-mar school" philosophy of the later Toronto branches, and Merritton, with its Gothic collegiate appearance, are among the other "non-classical" Ontario libraries. Goderich, in a category by itself, copies Victorian Ro-manesque with its steeply pitched roof and massive corner tower.

One of the most interesting buildings, quite unlike any other Car-negie library in Ontario, is the Pembroke library, ostensibly designed by Francis C. Sullivan of Ottawa in 1911-12. This building reflects the work of Frank Lloyd Wright, with its flat roof and projecting eaves distin-guishing it from the preferred neo-classic designs. Wright's "participation in [this] project was unofficial, and generally not known; consequently his name does not appear in any of the documents between the building committee and the architect."[14] However, the Pembroke Library is one of four buildings that Sullivan shared with Wright; although Sullivan prepared all working drawings and carried out the site supervision, Wright "justifiably acknowledges himself as designer."[15] This association began

Yorkville Branch, Toronto. *The Yorkville Branch library is quite similar in its classical design to many of the libraries in the small Ontario communities.*

Seaforth Carnegie library. *Seaforth is another of the beautiful small town Carnegie libraries.*

in 1907, when Sullivan left the office of E.L. Horwood (architect of the Ottawa Carnegie Library) and spent a year in Chicago at Wright's Oak Park Studio. Returning to Ottawa he spent three years as an architect with the federal Department of Public Works before starting his own practice, which continued from 1911 to 1917.[16] "His unyielding desire to produce the best possible building did not allow for any consideration of the builder or tradesman;" his site supervision was thorough, his standards extreme.[17] With declining work due to his "obstinate character," Sullivan left Ottawa in 1923, remaining in the employ of Wright at Taliesin until he died, a few years later.[18]

Walking through the primarily Victorian downtown area of Pembroke, the sight of the Carnegie Library, set up on a hill overlooking the town, comes as a distinct shock, particularly when one remembers the date that this magnificent building was completed, 1914. Sadly, the front doors and much of the interior detailing have disappeared, and only items such as the newel posts and the views through the windows serve as reminders of the ancestry of this remarkable library.

Independent of the architect, almost all the Ontario Carnegie libraries share one common feature: large windows responding to the need for natural light. One of the interesting functional requirements recommended by Bertram resulted in the small, high rear windows, which accommodated wall mounted bookshelves in many of the libraries. Mitchell, Walkerton, Lindsay, as well as the first Toronto branches are among those which have this element in common.

In a few library buildings pedimented windows were incorporated into the designs. At Brantford, the names of noted authors appearing on the window heads, added to the Latin inscription over the main door, "Exegi monumentum aere perennius," (translated "I have erected a monument more lasting than bronze") to give the building a desired cultural theme. In Fort William (now part of Thunder Bay) stained glass representations of the busts of similar authors appear in fan lights over the windows. Carnegie's picture was originally included in similar stained glass over the main entrance.

Four of the larger libraries, Sarnia, Guelph, Brantford, and Chatham had domes as a major design feature. In Brantford, the only survivor of these Carnegie libraries, the copper sheathed dome adds to the Palladian appearance of the building, with multi-paned windows in the drum allowing light to filter into the rotunda below. Woodstock has an internal dome not expressed on the exterior, with a rotunda defined by plaster columns with Corinthian capitals. Bertram, as could be expected, disliked domes, considering them wasteful ornamentation.

Stained glass was used in several of the early Carnegie libraries to add an additional air of quality to the appearance; the libraries at Guelph, Chatham and Ottawa, for example, were enriched in this way. Small designs, frequently of a lamp of learning, were often incorporated in the entrance fanlights. Other interesting or unique effects were provided by features such as the owls which guarded the St. Catharines Carnegie Library, as described earlier, or the urn at the apex of the New Liskeard Library pediment.

Classical detailing continued into the library interior, with ceiling heights usually ranging from 12 to 15 feet providing an environment which was sympathetic to the monumentality of the exterior. Wood, almost invariably local quarter-cut oak, southern pine, ash or maple and stained a dark hue, was used for the imposing counters and delivery desks and to face the columns and beams. In Windsor, the delivery desk

Art Nouveau plaque. *Details of the Frances Sullivan-Frank Lloyd Wright Carnegie library in Pembroke. The Wright details can be clearly identified from the carving of the newel post, the Mondrian-like design of the windows, and the Art Nouveau plaque.*

Mondrian-like window design.

Newel post.

Windows, Brantford Carnegie library. *The Brantford window heads with display of authors' names were matched in the Fort William Library, where busts of similar authors were depicted in the stained glass window heads on three sides of the building. The bust of Andrew Carnegie was originally in the fan light over the Fort William front door but was removed during modern renovations.*

Fort William Carnegie library.

was further enhanced by an old fashioned brass grill which separated the user from the library staff—and the books. In Waterloo, plastered partitions with wood wainscotting and windows of etched glass separated the men's and women's reading rooms from both the delivery hall and the stacks. Separate rooms for men and women were not unusual, particularly in the larger libraries: Berlin, St. Catharines or Brantford are other examples of libraries planned in this way.

Floors were most frequently oak wood strips, with mosaic tile in the more elaborate interiors such as Windsor's. Ceilings were either plaster or pressed metal, with decorated moldings framing the bays. Smiths Falls has a particularly beautiful rosette encircled by a be-ribboned garland and deep moldings in the centre of the ceiling. The library interiors, except in those few later buildings which followed Bertram's dictum for one large room, were divided by columns and archways, with classical capitals and decorative moldings. At Smiths Falls, the stairways were identified by free standing Ionic capped columns, topped by electric globes and finished with a delicate ballustrade. Mounted busts of authors graced the central halls of the St. Thomas and Windsor libraries.

Lighting in most of the libraries was provided by pendant, multi-headed fixtures that could be adapted either for acetylene gas or electricity. Heating was hot water or steam, through cast iron radiators located below windows and in stairwells. In some instances, such as Waterloo, mid-floor radiators were enclosed in ornamental cast-iron grillwork with a white marble slab top. Furnishings, for the most part, were wood, with heavy solid oak being favoured for reading room tables and chairs.

Although most of the Ontario libraries, with their main floor and high basement, had little need for elaborate stairways, the larger buildings such as Ottawa, Hamilton and Toronto all had grand staircases. Hamilton's double staircase with white marble ballustrade and handrail curved to the second floor. In Ottawa, a wooden handrail supported by wrought iron ballustrading followed the three sides of the rectangular stairwell, while heavy classical motifs graced the accompanying balcony. An observation balcony was included in the St. Thomas Library, allowing the Chief Librarian or Board member a view of the activity below. A hidden window in the mezzanine offices gave the Woodstock librarian similar opportunity.

Unfortunately, new suspended ceilings, fluorescent lighting and painted woodwork have robbed the interiors of most of the Ontario Carnegie libraries of their original charm. New Liskeard exists as an outstanding example of what once was, while the renovation of the Fort William Library restores much of the earlier period. The destruction of the earliest libraries has depleted the richness of the province's heritage. The Cornwall Carnegie Library had a semi-circular arched entrance with short columns, and a frivolous corner turret with a conical roof that made the building a gem. The Chatham, Sarnia and St. Catharines buildings (all demolished) provided their communities with a very special beauty which should not have been lost.

Sarnia Carnegie library. *Interiors of the early Carnegie libraries continued the classical detailing. The use of grill work in Berlin and Windsor to separate the public from the circulation desk is a feature that would be considered most inappropriate today.*

Windsor Carnegie library.

Berlin Carnegie library.

Waterloo Carnegie library.

Hamilton Carnegie library. *The interior of the Hamilton Public Library shows a lavish use of marble. The squared columns flanking the main staircase give way to the round columns defining the coffered ceiling.*

Table 11   Architects for more than two Carnegie Libraries

Architect	Libraries (by date)		
W.A. Mahoney	Fergus	Forest	Tillsonburg
	Campbellford	Port Hope	Fort Francis
	Aylmer	Whitby	Parkhill
	Durham	Watford	Stirling
	Elmira	Exeter	
W.E. Binning	Listowel	Harriston	Preston
	Hanover	Mitchell	Beaverton
	Teeswater	Ayr	
A.H. Chapman	Toronto Reference Library (with Wickson & Gregg)	Dundas	Barrie
George Gray	Grand Valley	Mount Forest	Walkerton
A.E. Nicholson	Thorold	Grimsby	Merritton

Architects

Not all architects for the Ontario Carnegie libraries have been identified, but the Carnegie Library Correspondence, early Library Board minutes, or local newspapers from the grant period reveal most of those involved. (These are listed in Appendix 4.) The work of two Ontario architects, Walter A. Mahoney of Guelph and W. E. Binning of Listowel, as mentioned, was most influential, with at least 22 of the 111 buildings designed between them (See Table 11). In addition, many of the other libraries were copied from their work through use of the plans collected by the Ontario Inspector of Libraries or the Ontario Library Association.

There seems little doubt that Bertram was not overly fond of architects, at least not those involved in designing libraries. Town Clerk E. Donnell of Barrie recognized this fact, when he wrote "I understand you do not want any correspondence with architects."[1] Bertram himself put it more directly to Board Secretary James Aitchison of Grimsby: "Everything should not hav been left to the architect, who as a rule, hav as their object to increase their reputation by a pretty bilding and subordinate the utilitarian."[2]

Ontario communities thought much more highly of their architects, referring to them as "reliable or most suitable," and most communities negotiated with several before they made their choice. It was not unusual for a Board or Council to ask several architects to submit plans and then select the one whose plans they liked best—or which they could afford. The Elmira archives, for example, contain complete plans prepared for the Board by J. A. Russell of Stratford, who received no recompense when the Board chose Mahoney's design for the Elmira Carnegie Library.

Welland was one of the most ambitious communities in terms of securing advice from a large number of architects, although this action did not particularly please Bertram. In April, 1914 the Welland Mayor, John Goodwin, sent Bertram a list of architects who he had asked to submit "preliminary sketches:"

B. F. Forbes, Welland
T. L. Nichols, Welland
Shepard & Calvin, Toronto
Palmer, Hornbostel & Jones
W. Herbert Dale, New York
W. Grayson Brown, Hamilton
Langman & Williams, Toronto
A. E. Nicholson, St. Catharines
D. J. Corrigail, Port Colborne
John Edmund Walker, Toronto

Bertram responded:

> Where did you get your list of architects? I do not recognize any one of them as ever having erected any library buildings about the size of your proposed one . . . A firm which has erected many important structures may or may not hav gained any experience to enable them to meet your case effectively and economically.[3]

Besides, all the architectural activity (many wrote or sent proposed sketches directly to Bertram) came to naught when the people of Welland defeated a library support by-law in 1914. Efforts to secure a Carnegie grant were

Elora Carnegie library. *Elora was designed by local architect William F. Sheppard, after objections from Bertram were overruled. Sheppard proved that he could design a classical building not unlike those by Walter Mahoney.*

Fort Frances Carnegie library. *In the most northerly of Architect Mahoney's libraries, he appears to have modified the "classical" detailing of the portico through the introduction of a broken architrave.*

renewed in 1919, at which time Norman A. Kearns of Welland was selected as architect and the library was completed, with no questions of architectural competence raised by Bertram.

Elora was among the communities which used a local architect for their Carnegie library—in spite of criticism from Bertram:

> We should like to know what experience your architect had in drawing plans of Library Buildings. Give us the names of places for which he has drawn plans. In the plans you sent he has made the delivery hall and steps take up a third of the building. From the first step in to where accommodation begins is about 25 feet. Your building itself is only 24 feet broad . . . Your architect does not show that he has had any experience at all with drawing Library plans.[4]

Elora Reeve A.J. Kerr defended their architect in determined fashion:

> In reply [we] beg to state that our Architect Mr. W.F. Sheppard spent some time with Mr. J.H. Adamson of New York and also at the Pratt Institute and for several years has had practical experience in Building in Brooklyn. As to actual Library Buildings, the Ontario Government gives plans and descriptions of every Library Building put up in this Province. We therefore feel that Mr. Sheppard is capable of providing plans suitable for a building and supervising same to meet the requirements of this town and we hope to your ultimate satisfaction. As he is a native of this place we feel like giving him a fair chance.[5]

Compromises were made in the size of the delivery hall and other features which Bertram had criticized, and Sheppard was allowed to continue in his position as Elora's architect.

A requirement for certification as an architect was not essential in order to have plans accepted by the Carnegie Corporation. The architect for the Shelburne Library was Dr. J. A. McKenzie, M.A., Ph.D., the local Presbyterian minister. He had previously distinguished himself by winning a contest for the design of the Shelburne Post Office and so was selected to do the Library as well. Dr. McKenzie fared no better at the hands of James Bertram than did most Ontario architects. Several sketch plans were returned for revision before the elevations and interior layouts received official sanction.

Analysis of the planning stage of the Carnegie library buildings leads to the conclusion that exact cost estimation was not a strength of the Ontario architects in the first decade of the twentieth century. The first architect for the Smiths Falls Library, M. McBride of London, Ontario, submitted plans for the $11,000 grant in 1902, which were $8,000 over that amount when the tenders were opened. His second set of plans was also well over the budget and his work was abandoned. Having failed twice with McBride the Smiths Falls Board chose a new architect in 1903, G. M. Bayley of Ottawa, whose plans were tendered and the building constructed for less than the grant amount![6]

W. E. Binning had problems with estimates for the Beaverton Library which drew severe criticism from Bertram. The Beaverton Library Board had selected Binning as their architect because they particularly liked the library he had designed for Mitchell—complete with small tower. The Mitchell plans with a few changes made by Binning were submitted to Bertram for approval, but this was not forthcoming. Moreover, the plans called for expenditures of $8,000, well above the $5,000 grant. After months

Shelburne Carnegie library. *The designer for this library was the local Presbyterian minister.*

of negotiation Bertram agreed to raise the grant to $7,000 and approved Binning's revised plans on the usual condition that the building be constructed according to the plans submitted, "complete and redy to occupy." Bertram was extremely annoyed, therefore, to receive a request from Beaverton for an additional $1,000 just eight months later, in January, 1913, with an explanatory letter from Binning to the Library Board enclosed, as follows:

> Yours to hand re application to Mr. Carnegie for a supplementary grant of $1,000 to finish up your building. I feel sorry that you should have to bother Mr. Carnegie's agents again, but as you say prices have taken such a rise lately that one hardly knows how to estimate. I am just now asking for tenders on a couple of Schools and find it very difficult to secure bids, so many of our best mechanics have gone west where there are greater attractions, and then the price of material is continually soaring. I trust now that everything has turned out so satisfactory so far as your people being so well pleased with the building that you may be able to secure the grant and that it may be finished up in good shape in every particular.[7]

Not surprisingly Bertram refused the extra money in no uncertain terms:

> When the lowest tender for the base structure was $6275 you made a contract in the full knowledge that the bilding complete and redy to occupy would cost very much more than the $7000 promist, notwithstanding the fact that the plans were only passed on the distinct understanding that the cost of the bilding complete and redy to occupy was to be within $7000. Mr. Carnegie under the circumstances does not feel called upon to accede to your request for further payment.[8]

Fees varied. Binning had a basic fee of $100, later increased to $125, in addition to $3.00 for each visit to the community (he estimated ten or twelve visits for a normal job). Mahoney submitted a standard contract to each client in which he outlined his fee as five per cent of the contracted price. Sidney R. Badgley of Cleveland returned his fee for the St. Catharines Carnegie Library since he was a "native son," and John Finlayson of Seaforth returned his usual five per cent fee so that his home town could pay for the library site.

The highest fee uncovered was the $2,159 paid to Francis Sullivan for the Pembroke Library, but this large sum did not exchange hands without a lot of controversy. After negotiating for a Carnegie grant from 1907 until 1911, when the formal resolution of acceptance and pledge of maintenance was finally sent to Bertram, the Pembroke Council engaged Sullivan to design their library, as noted above. The first set of plans, without approval from Bertram, were sent out to tender and they returned at an estimated cost of $17,000, $5,000 over the promised grant. The Council asked Sullivan to revise the plans to a reduced scale, and these were then tendered at $12,995, with architectural fees and other expenses to be added. This new set of plans was sent to Bertram, by personal courier, and evoked a lengthy critical response which began abruptly with his observation that "the plans are very poor. As a matter of fact, more of effective accommodation could be secured for $12,000 than the architect has received in these plans for $14,000."[9]

So Sullivan revised the plans yet again and sent these to Bertram in June, 1912, with a letter which refuted most of Bertram's criticisms.

Mitchell Carnegie library. *Architect Binning copied his Listowel plans for Mitchell, using red brick instead of grey precast concrete blocks for the exterior walls.*

Listowel Carnegie library.

This exchange only annoyed Bertram further, and he charged angrily that Sullivan did not "seem to be familiar with planning libraries." Sullivan was not prepared to accept such criticism with humility:

> That portion of your letter re my not being familiar with Library Planning is debateable [sic].
> I quite understand that I have to conform to your interpretation of this matter in hand of Planning, and am quite willing to do so, and render you my best effort and it is above mediocrity.
> I have no "grouch" or "kick" to make re your criticisms as long as they will lead to your conclusions and are fair to me.[10]

Since Pembroke had only been promised a grant of $12,000 and the final plans were still projected at $14,000, it was two more years before the Pembroke Town Council had satisfied Bertram that an increase to $14,000, $2,000 over the original grant promise, was appropriate. In January, 1914, Franks was authorized to accept certificates for payment and by October of that year, with the building near completion, Sullivan submitted to Pembroke Council a summary of all costs associated with the building. This amount included, in addition to the contract price of $14,687, architectural fees as follows:

```
Abandoned drawings:
    Set no. 1.................................................$  646.00
    Set no. 2.................................................$  524.24
Accepted design..............................................$  988.93
    Total fees: .............................................$2,159.17[11]
```

The Council paid the architect's fees as presented and sent the bill for recovery to Franks. A response from Bertram, not Franks, was swift and to the point. "I beg to inform you," he wrote a mere two weeks later, "that this Corporation can only include in payments for any one bilding payments for architect's commission on but one set of plans."[12] Since Pembroke's payment to Sullivan had put the Town over the $14,000 grant by $1,657.83, Bertram was justifiably annoyed. He further asked where Pembroke planned to get the money, and stated firmly that "it is unheard of for an architect to charge two commisions for the preparation of plans for any of the library bildings which this Corporation provides."[13]

So it would appear that Pembroke was left to pay the extra cost and the Town soon discovered that their architect could be firm in other matters as well. Mayor J.L. Morris received the following letter, with Sullivan's "characteristic lack of tact,"[14] just prior to the opening of the new building:

> We have been advised that your LIBRARIAN has instructed that the Equipment as planned and designed by us re above noted Building has been changed to suit her whims, etc. inasmuch as the Equipment is being placed other than shown on plans accepted by Carnegie Corporation, and that her desires have been carried out by your Committee. Just advise your Committee and the LIBRARIAN that the equipment must be placed as designed and shown on Plans, no other way will be accepted, and if this is not acceptable to the LIBRARIAN, remove the LIBRARIAN. Why? Because outside of the arrangement as shown I do not want the load of several thousand volumes concentrated over an area not designed to sustain that which was intended being distributed as planned over the entire area. Now both the structural and

plan arrangement are more important than the fear of a draft blowing upon the LIBRARIAN, and I trust that you will see the importance of my directions in this matter being carried out, otherwise I will not finally pass the Building for clearance to the Carnegie Corporation. I am very sorry indeed that consideration should be given to such a whimsical and awkward suggestion by a person not familar with the requirements as re Equipment and structural requirements. Again, any other arrangement would conflict with the architectural feature of the arrangement of fixtures or Equipment in question.[15]

Although Sullivan was prepared to accept any challenge, as both the bold library in Pembroke and his letters attest, most other architects were more complacent and accepted Bertram's criticisms without argument. J. A. McKenzie of Shelburne wrote in 1911 to Andrew Carnegie:

Re public library. The Board here asked me to prepare plans for a new building. I drew a rough sketch which I believe was forwarded to you and was not accepted. I am naturally interested in the success of this project and if you would please let me know what you require I would gladly comply.[16]

Unfortunately his answer came from Bertram, not Carnegie, who was his usual obtuse self: "Did you get the 'Notes on Library Bilding' which was supplied to the secretary of the Library Board? If you did, study them and then see if your sketch plans are in accord with the ideas exprest therein."[17] McKenzie persevered, without argument, until his plans were finally considered acceptable.

If Bertram's directions were simple—follow the floor plans provided in his "Notes,"—Toronto's Locke felt that the role of the architect called for much more. His views of library architecture, which were expressed in an architectural journal at the end of the two decades of Carnegie library building, provide a synthesis of the experience which had been gained and the challenges still to be met in planning and building libraries.

Library architecture in Canada is in its infancy and there are endless opportunities for architects of the future who posess a vigorous imagination and a passion for breaking new ground, in following up this interesting branch of the profession. The types of library architecture which were in vogue during the last part of the past century and the first decade of the twentieth century are now distinctly passee—and justly so. Their early decline is due largely to the fact that library ideals have undergone radical change within the last decade, and the natural result of this changed conception of the scope and method of library work is that the phlegmatic buildings of the past are no longer suitable for the successful undertaking of professional library service.[18]

He went on to describe the rapid development of library work for children, the introduction of "Story Hours", the need for club and lecture rooms, and then called for changes to meet the new challenges:

The library building which endeavours to meet the requirements of this new conception of librarianship must be above all, adaptable. It must take into consideration the fact that library work is not static but dynamic, and it must be of such a shape and style that an extension could be added without destroying the symmetry of the building.

It must be conceived by an imaginative brain, for adaptability is impossible without imagination. The architect must realize that he is not called upon to plan a mere house for books—but an intellectual home for the community. The Public Library is tending more and more to become the social centre of the community and it should express this fact in its architecture. It should possess a personality in keeping with its environment, and, like a painting, should be a glorified expression of the tastes and characteristics of the community, rather than a photographic likeness.

An architect who would design a satisfactory building for a modern community library has an interesting task before him, and one which is by no means easy. Not only must he take all the foregoing ideas into consideration; the personality of the library, its adaptability, the various phases of the work which it essays to do, but he must always bear in mind that the windows, radiators, and ventilation must be so arranged to give a maximum of wall space for book shelves, since floor stacks are ugly and make the problems of lighting and administration more difficult. He must juggle in somehow a lecture room, a Children's room and an Adult reading room without placing either in the basement. Yet he must remember that ground space costs money, and also that a certain proportion of the lot must be reserved for an attractive setting. With all of these considerations kept in mind a satisfactory building could be erected at a moderate cost, but not without taxing the ingenuity of the architect to a considerable degree.[19]

The task which Locke so ably described in 1926 is not that different today, with technological developments and concern about operating costs adding to the complexity.

Construction and costs

Most communities followed standard practices of advertising for tenders, although contemporary records that have survived cannot confirm that a public notice was in all cases submitted to newspapers. An early example of such a notice appeared in Windsor's *Evening Record*:

Notice to Contractors.

Windsor Public Library.

Sealed tenders addressed to A. Phi. E. Panet, chairman of Building Committee, Windsor Public Library Board, Windsor, Ont., will be received until 4 p.m. Monday, 5th day of May, 1902, for the different contracts connected with the new library building to be erected in Windsor. Each tender must be accompanied by a certified cheque, payable to the order of A. Phi E. Panet, chairman of building committee, to the amount of 5 per cent of the tender, to guarantee that the successful bidder, if awarded the contract, will accept the same and furnish the required bonds. Contractors must in their tender state the number of working days they require to complete their work. And they may, if they choose, tender for the complete building.

Plans and specifications may be seen on and after Tuesday, the 22nd day of April, 1902, at my office in the Curry block Ouellette-ave Windsor, Ontario.

Essex Carnegie library. *Use of field stone for the foundation wall was unusual in Ontario. This side view of the Essex library also shows a stone band course at first floor level, and brackets at the eaves, not continued on the rear of the building.*

Fort Frances Carnegie library, laying of the cornerstone, 1914. *The stone lintels over the basement windows and the first level floor joists were already in place when town officials came to lay the cornerstone.*

The right to reject any or all tenders reserved.

Dated at Windsor, Ont., April 18th 1902.

A. Phi. E. Panet,
Chairman Building Committee.[1]

A more detailed tender document for the proposed additions to the Berlin Library, 1916, has been preserved in the Library archives. Instructions for the various trades included the following:

Firring.
Provide and fix all centres, templates, turning pieces, blocks, 3/8" x 4" strips, bond timbers, wood, brick, brackets for coves, including to present part of the new Children's Room, brackets for beams, etc. as required by the work shown or specified. Material for all rough carpentry work shall be pine or spruce.

Lintels.
All openings to have cambered lintels, 2" deep for each foot of span of opening, with proper wall hold, except where steel beams are shown.

Partitions.
Main plastered partition shown in Librarian's room to be of 2" x 6" studs, cupboard partition 2" x 4" all sized. Double studs at openings and wherever necessary. Properly frame and brace. Cut in one row of horizontal bridging between studs.

Window frames.
Windows in new wing will be double hung standard box frames, similar in construction and detail to those of present building. Old frames where reused as indicated to be made good where necessary, and sash hung with new cord etc. The main windows on First floor to have dentilled transoms as shown with hinged transom sash above. All sliding sash to be hung with Sampson spot cord or equal with anti-friction pulleys and cast iron weights. All frames are to have a rough piece on back as directed to insure wind joint. Window in Librarian's room to be casement window with transom and mullion as shown.[2]

Whenever a community asked for additional funds to complete a library or to build an addition, Bertram asked for details of the expenditure of the original grant. The Chairman of the Guelph Library Board, James Watt, sent the following letter when Guelph was requesting an additional grant of $4000 to finish that library in 1904:

Answering your letter to the Secretary of the Library Board, I enclose herein a statement showing how the original grant has been expended, and what the increased appropriation would be used for.
I give some explanation of the cause of the extras. There may yet be some claims by the various contractors for extras, but we do not anticipate any claim over and above an amount which the Board themselves can finance.[3]

151

Included with this letter was a detailed statement of expenditures and the proposed appropriation.

Statement for Andrew Carnegie, Esq.
Shewing Appropriation of his Grant to Guelph Public Library

		Extras
Tenders for Masonry ...	$5000....	$675.
Carpentry	3985.	
Artificial Stone	5400.	
Plastering	607.....	190.
Heating	1000.....	706.
Roofing	190.	
Plumbing	300.	
Tinsmithing	135.	
Painting & Glazing	525.....	135.
Lighting Fixtures	285.	
Wiring	210.	
Corner Stone	25.	
Architect	1000.	
	$18637.	$1715.
		18637.
		$20352.

Appropriation .... $20000.
Balance over expended 352.00

Notes re extras

Masonry	.............$675.	.........Architect omitted cementing some walks, cellars, covering of dome, steel rails for strengthening arches, expanded metal in dome.
Plastering	............$190.	.........The cost of heating the building.
Heating	..............$700.	.........Increase by substituting hot water for steam.
Painting	.............$135.	.........Tenderer became insolvent and next man's figure that much higher.

Proposed appropriation of $4000. additional

To pay above overdraft	$352.
Cork Carpet Tender	165.
Delivery Counter	100.
Furniture, new, including steel stacks, per tenders	2998.
Tiling lavatories and entrance (tender)	351.65

To complete interior entrance (in addition to what is called for by original plans)

Plastering (tender)	472.
Carpenter (tender)	350.
Inscribed bronze tablet	50.
	$4838.65

Window blinds
Storm windows
Fixing of Grounds

Comments by Bertram on the main cause of the cost over-run—"omissions by the architect"—would have proved interesting. Unfortunately, there are none in the files.

Amherstburg Carnegie library. *Beautiful examples of the few stone Carnegie libraries in the province of Ontario.*

New Liskeard Carnegie library.

With no exception the exterior walls of the Ontario Carnegie libraries were built in load bearing masonry: stone, brick or precast stone. Foundation walls enclosing the exposed basements were often built in stone or precast stone up to the first floor level, or to the level of the main entrance. Local stone was commonly used for these foundation walls so that Campellford, located in a Canadian Shield area made use of granite, whereas New Liskeard, Amherstburg and St. Marys used local limestone.

First and second floor wall materials were for the most part brick— either buff or varieties of red. A few buildings such as St. Marys, Amherstburg, Fergus and New Liskeard were built entirely of dressed stone ("rock faced coursed ashlar") complete with stone lintels, quoins and keystones. Penetanguishene combined both stone and buff brick on its front facade.

A detailed description of building materials was included in the discussion of the Lindsay Carnegie Library in the 1906 Report of the Public Library Inspector:

> The rubble stone for the masonry was obtained at Cobo conk, the course ashlar above grade line was obtained at Britnell & Co.'s quarries at Burnt River, and cannot be excelled in appearance and quality. The brickwork is of red stack brick laid with American bond in brown mortar. The window sills, architraves, and quoins and columns are of artificial stone, which add greatly to the appearance of the building. The fireplaces are built of No. 1 red pressed brick. The whole of the carpenter work is of clear pine lumber.[4]

Choice of exterior building material had important implications for the final cost of the library. The Guelph prices (shown above) for a $24,500 stone building in 1904, can be compared with those for the primarily brick library in Collingwood, 1905.

Statement of cost of Public Library building contracts (Collingwood)

Eli Holmes, Stone & Brick work	$ 5105.38
Wilson Bros., Carpenter Work	4312.65
F. Hectomore, Electric Wiring	301.58
R.H. Munson, Painting & Glazing	509.00
John Lockten, Plastering	547.00
Bennett & Wright, Plumbing & Heating	1558.00
Thos. Irwin & Sons, Slating & Iron Works	1308.35
W.& W. Stewart, Architects' fees	551.90
John Chamberlain, Inspector of works	210.00
Total cost	$14803.86[5]

Costs of furnishings also provide revealing insight into the industrial environment of an earlier time. The St. Marys Library Board received the following quote on their furnishings from The Office Specialty Manufacturing Co. Ltd. of Toronto.

> We understand that you will require about six hundred feet of shelving. For this you would require about 228 Sectional Bookcases, as each case is 34" wide outside. This would give you 38 stacks each 6 sections high, and we would be pleased to supply you with:

38 standard Bases,
38 sections, 13¼" high inside
76 sections, 11¼" high inside
ll4 sections, 9¼" high inside
38 Cornices.
for Six Hundred and Forty-Five Dollars ($645.00).

4 Tables, each 8 ft. × 4 ft.
1 Table, 5 ft. × 2 ft. 8 in.
1 Table, 4 ft. × 2 ft. 8 in.
40 small Chairs, #101.
10 Arm Chairs, #102.
for Two Hundred and Ninety-five Dollars ($295.00).

The bookcases and the tables and chairs would all be finished in Golden Oak or any other finish that you might desire.

If you decide to have steel shelving in place of Sectional Bookcases, we will be pleased to quote you on:

600 ft. of shelving, in either double or single stacks, without cornice, but finished standards, as per drawing #269 . $650.00

Same amount of shelving, with cornice top, as per drawing #268 or #270 .... $900.00

The steel stacks would be constructed of the best cold rolled, pickled steel, finished with three heavy coats of the best enamel baked to 350:

These prices include freight and cost of setting up, where necessary.

We are enclosing you blueprints illustrating the steel stacks, the style of tables as quoted on and the chairs and sectional bookcases, and trust that our quotation may be found satisfactory and we will guarantee that the goods will meet with the approval of the architect and of your Library Board.[6]

Sarnia Carnegie library.

Chapter Four

Ontario Carnegie libraries

Where they are—and were

Only two American states, Indiana and California, received more Carnegie grants, 164 and 142 respectively, than the province of Ontario. Of the 111 buildings originally constructed with Carnegie support in Ontario, seventy-nine continue to be used as libraries although few—most notably the New Liskeard Library—do so without some renovation. Maps 1-4 shows the location of the original and remaining libraries, while Tables 12-14 list them.

Unfortunately, fifteen of the buildings as shown in Table 13 were demolished to make way for new construction, or were destroyed by fire.

Another seventeen buildings no longer serve as libraries, as per Table 14, but have been converted for other uses, most frequently still serving a civic function such as the Department of Engineering in St. Thomas, or the Police Department in Waterloo.

Table 12   Remaining Carnegie Libraries in Ontario (1983)

Amherstburg	Glencoe	New Hamburg	Smiths Falls
Ayr	Goderich	New Liskeard	Stirling
Barrie	Grand Valley	Norwich	Stratford
Beaverton	Gravenhurst	Norwood	Tavistock
Bracebridge	Grimsby	Orangeville	Teeswater
Brantford	Hanover	Orillia	Thorold
Brockville	Harriston	Ottawa West	Toronto —
Brussels	Hespler	Branch	Yorkville
Campbellford	Ingersol	Owen Sound	Riverdale
Clinton	Kemptville	Palmerston	Wychwood
Dresden	Kenora	Paris	High Park
Durham	Kincardine	Parkhill	Beaches
Elmira	Kingsville	Pembroke	Annette
Elora	Lindsay	Penetanguishene	Walkerton
Essex	Listowel	Picton	Wallaceburg
Exeter	Lucknow	Port Elgin	Watford
Fergus	Markdale	Port Hope	Welland
Forest	Merritton	Renfrew	Weston
Fort Francis	Milverton	St. Marys	Woodstock
Fort William	Mitchell	Seaforth	
(Thunder Bay)	Mount Forest	Shelburne	

Table 13   Carnegie library buildings destroyed

Chatham	Leamington	Sarnia
Collingwood	Mimico (Etobicoke)	Sault Ste. Marie
Cornwall	North Bay	St. Catharines
Guelph	Oshawa	Tillsonburg
Kitchener (Berlin)	Ottawa (Main)	Windsor

Table 14   Carnegie buildings no longer used as libraries (1983)

Aylmer	Niagara Falls	Stouffville
Brampton	Perth	Toronto Reference Library
Dundas	Peterborough	Toronto:
Galt	Preston	Queen and Lisgar Branch
Hamilton	Simcoe	Waterloo
Midland	St. Thomas	Whitby

Map One. *The province of Ontario in relationship to Canada and the United States.*

158

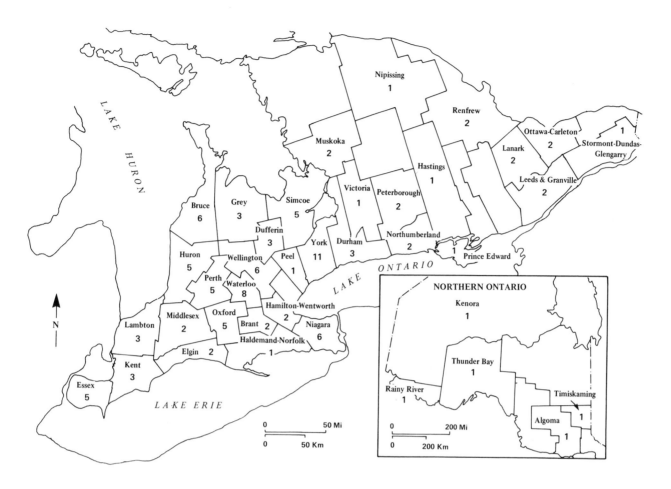

Map Two. *Distribution of Carnegie libraries by County.*

CARNEGIE LIBRARIES

● STILL IN USE

○ DEMOLISHED

■ OTHER USE

N

0   10   20 Mi

0   10   20   30 Km

Penetanguishene ■ Midland

Orillia ●

● Owen Sound

○ Collingwood

● Port Elgin

● Barrie

● Markdale

■ Stouffville

● Kincardine   Hanover
                    ● Durham

● Walkerton   ● Shelburne

● Teeswater   ● Mount Forest

Lucknow   Harriston   ● Orangeville   Toronto ●

                ● Palmerston   ● Grand Valley   Brampton ■   ■ Toronto Central
                                                              ● Yorkville
Brussels   Elora   ■ Queen and Lisgar
● Goderich   ● Listowel   ● Fergus   Mimico ○   ● Riverdale
                                                              ● Wychwood
● Clinton   Milverton   ● Elmira   ● High Park
  ● Seaforth   ○ Guelph   ● Beaches
● Mitchell   Waterloo Berlin   ● Toronto Junction
              New Hamburg ○ ● Hespeler   ● Weston
  Stratford ●   ■ Preston
            ● Tavistock ■ Galt   ● Hamilton
Exeter ●   ● Ayr   Grimsby ●
      ● St. Marys   Paris ●   Dundas ■   ● Merritton
● Parkhill   ● Brantford   St. Catharines ● ○ Niagara
● Forest   Thorold ● ■ Falls
                ● Woodstock
○ Sarnia   ● Watford   ● Ingersoll   ● Welland
                         ● Norwich

                Tillsonburg
                    ○   ■ Simcoe
● Glencoe   ■ Alymer
          St. Thomas ■

Wallaceburg
● Dresden
    ● Chatham

○ Windsor
  ● Essex
● Amherstburg ○ Leamington
Kingsville ●

Map Three. *Southwestern and Central Ontario, with location of Carnegie libraries.*

160

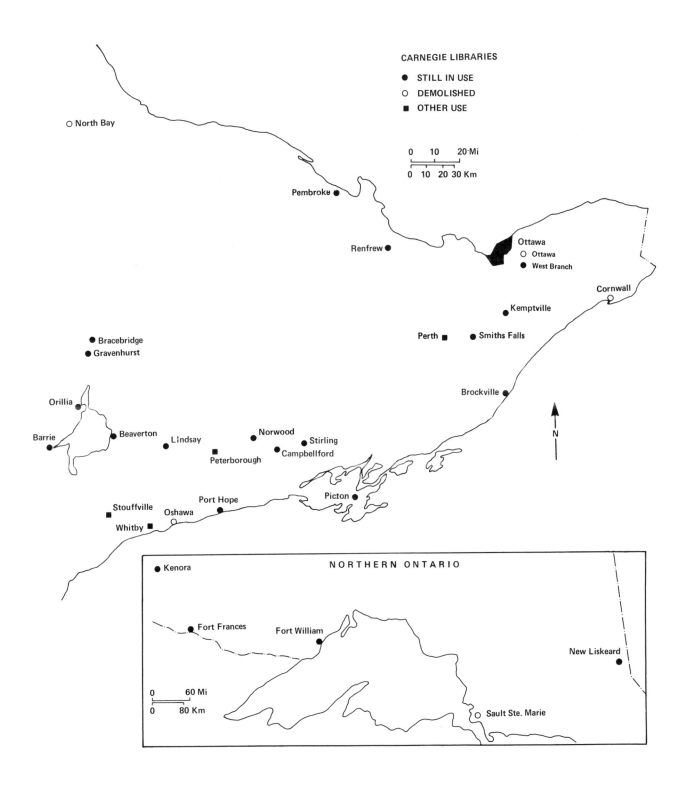

● STILL IN USE
○ DEMOLISHED
■ OTHER USE

○ North Bay

Pembroke ●

Renfrew ●

Ottawa
○ Ottawa
● West Branch

Cornwall ○

Kemptville ●

Perth ■   ● Smiths Falls

Brockville ●

● Bracebridge
● Gravenhurst

Orillia ●

Barrie ●

Beaverton ●   Lindsay ●   ● Norwood   ● Stirling

■   ● Campbellford
Peterborough

N

Port Hope ●

Stouffville ■   Oshawa   Picton ●
Whitby ■   ○

NORTHERN ONTARIO

● Kenora

● Fort Frances   Fort William ●

New Liskeard ●

0   60 Mi

0   80 Km

Sault Ste. Marie ○

Map Four. *Southeastern and Northern Ontario, with location of Carnegie libraries.*

161

North Bay Carnegie library. *One of the fifteen Ontario Carnegie buildings which no longer exist.*

Niagara Falls Carnegie library. *One of the seventeen buildings no longer used as a library, the Niagara Falls Carnegie building is currently used by Community Services.*

Services

A record of the Carnegie libraries would be incomplete without some description of the collections and services that were available in Ontario in the first years of their operation. A few of the Library Boards or Town Councils preserved some record of their Carnegie Library activities in letters, either to Carnegie or Bertram. Andrew Braid wrote from Windsor a year after their new building opened in 1903, that:

> I am as proud as a piper at our new building; and altho it has increased my library work (which has to be done in the evenings and after office hours), I am more than repaid at the knowledge that the number of readers and the circulation of books have increased greatly. We allow unrestricted access to the stack room, and it is a fine sight to see the number of people scattered among the shelves, selecting or examining the books. We find an improvement in our readers' tastes—less fiction and more of the general works being taken now. From my heart I thank you for your gift to Windsor, and I am proud to have been the means of interesting you in the matter.[1]

The Hanover Town Council appointed a special Committee to thank Bertram officially, after their Library opened, and it reported on their library's increased use as well:

> The building itself and the purposes for which it was built is highly appreciated by the public, as the following figures will show. The average monthly visitors to the Reading Room since the building is in use is not less than fifteen hundred (1500), and the books charged each month amount to eight hundred (800). This represents a gain in the Reading Room of about 90%, and in the distribution of books of about 125%, which is most gratifying.[2]

Such letters in the Carnegie correspondence are few. Fortunately, the annual reports which had to be submitted to the Inspector of Public Libraries if a government grant were to be obtained provide a cross-section of library services in the early Carnegie libraries.

By 1906 some twenty Carnegie libraries had been completed, most with a stack room that could be kept closed to the general public, or to some category of it. Both large and small libraries denied such access to books, for example Ottawa, St. Catharines, Waterloo, St. Marys and Collingwood. Other libraries, such as Berlin, St. Thomas and Stratford, allowed free access except to the fiction collections, whereas others restricted access by age. Paris had an age limit of fourteen years, Waterloo's was twelve, while St. Thomas regulations stated that: "Normally children under twelve are not permitted to take out books, but in reality the matter is left to the discretion of the librarian."[3] Windsor was even stricter and their age limit was sixteen, but the Librarian was given discretionary power. Berlin solved this problem by allowing parents to take out cards and books for their children. Many libraries, however, did give free access to all collections: Paris, Picton, Guelph, Chatham, Bracebridge and Harriston were examples of this more advanced thinking.

Card catalogues were fast becoming popular by 1906, and many libraries were switching from printed catalogues for part or all of their collection. Similarly, most libraries were either using or planning to use the Dewey Decimal classification, which had been developed in 1876 in the United States, and was being encouraged by the Inspector of Public Libraries for Ontario public libraries. St. Thomas reported in 1906 that: "Our librarian was this summer sent to Boston, Mass., to learn the Dewey System, and this system is now being introduced. We intend to have a printed catalogue for the books in fiction, and an indicator to show whether they are in or out. Books in fiction will be numbered according to the Cutter table. For books other than fiction we intend to use the Card Catalogue and the Dewey classification."[4]

Stratford had similar plans, but described their existing system as follows: "The shelf grouping is in 12 sections, biography, poetry and religion being classified by author, history and travel by country alphabetically, physics and science by sub-section under title. The Dewey system will replace the present system at an early date."[5]

Children's library services had been recognized in a very few of the early Carnegie libraries. Waterloo reported on a catalogue for children as did Berlin, while Guelph's special effort was: "Two large tables provided with bound volumes of illustrated periodicals are placed in the general reading room for the use of children."[6] The Sarnia report described the most advanced service for children in any Ontario Carnegie Library to that date:

> Special attention is devoted to library work for children.
> Books suitable for children in every department of literature have been freely purchased. The assistant librarian has been given special charge of children's work.
> A story hour has been inaugurated by the children's librarian.
> Stories are told to the children so as to interest them in great men, or events, and in nature study, science, etc. The children are told what books are in the library dealing with the subject of the story, and encouraged to read for themselves.
> The policy of the Board has not been to send out Travelling Libraries to the schools, but to bring the children to the library.
> The Board has secured the co-operation of the teachers who make lists suitable for the different forms. Copies of these lists are given to the children's librarian, and to the scholars in each form, and form part of the school curriculum.[7]

Emphasis placed on this special service to children resulted in rapid changes. In 1906 Ottawa reported that their Library contained a Children's room with special books and that the Library "cooperated with local schools." By 1909 this service had increased to a separate card catalogue and circulation system for the children, and in addition:

> Special efforts are being made to co-operate with the schools. Collections of books are sent from the library to the Collegiate Institute and several of the larger public schools. Negotiations are also on foot with the Separate School Board looking toward a similar arrangement. It is hoped that in time a complete system of small libraries will be installed in the public, separate and high schools of Ottawa through the public library. The librarian has issued a special teacher's card, entitling the holder to take ten books at a time and keep them for a month. This privilege applies to all teachers in Ottawa schools of every description, public and private, and also to the students in the Normal School.[8]

A variety of other special services were mentioned in the 1906 reports, including German books in Berlin and special meetings of the Historical Society in Lindsay. Sarnia described the most variation in their cultural activities:

> The auditorium may be used by any body of a public or semipublic nature, without charge. The Historical Society, The Children's Aid Society, The Medical Association, The Camera Club and other Societies regularly meet in this room.
>
> The Smoking room is supplied with newspapers and tables for chess and checkers are provided."[9]

St. Thomas also had an active programme: an auditorium seating 300 persons was used for meetings of an "educational character." Typical of these was a lecture by "William Wilfrid Campbell, Canadian poet," two weeks after the Library opened in February 1906.[10]

For many of the communities, the increased facilities and opportunities for more than the mere lending of a few books which the Carnegie libraries provided presented a major challenge. Regulations for library use, cataloguing and classification systems, monitoring of auditorium or lecture rooms, training for library staff, were all issues which had to be handled, many for the first time. Guidance provided by the Inspector of Public Libraries and by the Ontario Library Association encouraged communities to expand library services to match the handsome new Carnegie buildings. Financial support, however, remained a problem and resulted in great variations in the number of books or other services available. Table 15, which includes data from some of the earliest Carnegie libraries, illustrates some of these differences.

Table 15   Free Public Library Statistics, 1906[11]

Community	Population 1901 census	Legislative grant $	Municipal grant $	No. of volumes	No. of periodicals	Circulation
Berlin	9,747	250.00	1,968.	7,918	72	11,386
Brampton	2,748	138.09	550.	4,719	23	13,845
Chatham	9,068	180.54	1,220.	6,713	39	21,773
Collingwood	5,755	96.08	1,450.	5,432	45	12,816
Cornwall	6,704	76.83	500.	3,717	44	14,045
Goderich	4,158	106.44	690.	4,327	48	12,214
Guelph	11,496	250.00	2,060.	10,102	54	54,725
Sarnia	8,176	250.00	1,991.	5,514	61	29,110
Smiths Falls	5,155	185.06	1,100.	4,497	45	17,116
Stratford	9,959	250.00	1,200.	7,516	48	38,185
St. Catharines ...	9,946	250.00	2,500.	9,398	65	28,148
Waterloo	3,537	204.90	802.	8,178	32	9,097
Windsor	12,153	250.00	3,500.	13,241	76	47,749

Library collections, as might be expected, were very small in the early years of the Ontario Carnegie libraries, with most libraries containing one book for each citizen—or fewer. Waterloo was the only community that approached modern standards of two or more books per capita. Use of the collections, as measured by circulation figures, is also interesting, in that the Guelph usage is so much higher than in other libraries. This might be explained by the fact that Guelph was the first free public library in Ontario under the 1882 Act,[12] or by differing library regulations—fiction did not circulate in all libraries, for example.

Books could be purchased for as little as fifty cents each, and only a few hundred new books were added to most collections each year. Assistance was provided in the selection of appropriate titles through the Department of Education, which recommended that the American Library Association catalogue of 7,520 titles be used since it was considered to be "indispensable as a guide in selecting books."[13] The Ontario Library Association also provided book lists for both adults and children, "as an aid to the smaller libraries without trained librarians."[14] Public Library Inspector Leavitt was concerned about the development of the collections in the public libraries, noting that in 1906 the purchase of fiction consumed as much as 75 per cent of some libraries' book budgets. He recommended that the Minister of Education be empowered to reduce that percentage to 45 per cent.[15]

Staffing was also a problem in the Carnegie libraries in their early years. Nursey reported in 1909 that he hoped to begin a summer school for library training in Toronto, similar to the one at McGill University, but this was not seen, evidently, as an urgent need.[16] Library trustees assumed that they should be responsible for book selection, and that training for other library activities—purchasing, cataloguing, children's services and promotion—while desirable, was not essential. Library staff appointments tended to be made, therefore, for reasons other than technical or professional qualifications: political favouritism, relationship to board members, and religious affiliations were all influential in staff choices. The attitude generally held about library staff qualifications was best expressed at a 1911 Library Institute meeting held at Niagara Falls:

> It is very important to have a librarian with a high education but this is not all important. I would say it is more important to have a pleasant young lady as librarian, one who is enthusiastic in the literary work; also one who loves children. It is all the better if she has a good education, but in our small libraries we cannot always pay the price for education.[17]

To overcome these well-entrenched opinions, Inspector Nursey finally persuaded the Department of Education to fund a library training programme, and a five week summer course was begun in 1911 at the Toronto Model School, with one of Ontario's first professional librarians, Mabel Dunham of the Berlin Public Library, as instructor.[18] This course continued in the following summers, but failed to attract attendance from smaller urban and rural libraries as had been hoped.

Renovations

Most of the original Carnegie libraries have been renovated in some manner, whether it is through the addition of carpeting and paint as in the Waterloo and Essex County libraries, or through extensions of the original buildings. These additions frequently have been done with some attention to the original design or function; those in Elmira, Owen Sound and Barrie for example, have not seriously compromised the Carnegie buildings. Others, such as Orillia and Wallaceburg, have buried the Carnegie facade within modern glass and brick designs.

It is unfortunate that some of the perceived problems of contemporary Carnegie libraries came from Bertram's original concepts. Most serious was his insistence that the basement be designed so that it could be used for a lecture room, which resulted in extensive internal and/or external stairways leading to the main library floor. Access for senior citizens or handicapped persons is difficult if not impossible (for example, there are more than twenty steps from the sidewalk to the circulation desk at the Milverton Public Library). Moreover, the fixed wall shelving under high rear windows which Bertram favoured proved inadequate for growing collections within a few years, and an extension to the entire building was shown to be far more costly than expansion of a small stack room. At the same time it must be recognized that those libraries which followed Bertram's original direction for few or moveable partitions have found it much easier to adjust functions to accommodate modern library services.

Refurbishing the libraries to meet present building standards with respect to heating, lighting and air conditioning or to support new technology has also proven difficult—and costly. The Goderich Carnegie Library has sufficient space for library functions but the cost for new heating and wiring, storm windows, insulation and carpeting required to bring the total building to an acceptable condition is currently considered too high. Meanwhile the second floor of the Library remains empty.

Problems of operating the two or three storey libraries should also be mentioned, since the total floor area cannot justify the larger staff numbers required if supervision must be provided for a library function—such as children's services—on other than the main floor. Some of the smaller communities have solved this problem by retaining all library functions on the main floor, allowing the basement to be used for community services. In Dresden a ladies' group gathers regularly for quilting, senior citizens meet in Orangeville, Lucknow shares its space with municipal offices, whereas Penetanguishene has the police department and Seaforth a day nursery in their library basements. Another problem of the three storey libraries is the inadequate structural strength of the second floor. Waterloo, for example, found that its top storey did not meet building code requirements for bookstacks.

The one floor libraries are particularly successful where a centralized book selection and processing service is provided through membership in provincial, county or regional library systems. The Carnegie Library can then be retained as a library public service centre, with collections continuously replenished from the central pool of books, films, or records, and with Telex, or in the future, computer terminals, linking it to its neighbours in an expanded library and information network. Essex, Lambton and Waterloo Counties have extremely good examples of this solution.

Elmira Carnegie library. *An addition has extended the usefulness of the Elmira Carnegie library.*

Mitchell Carnegie library. *The high rear windows allowed wall shelving to be placed below, a feature much admired by Bertram.*

Fort William Carnegie library. *Now the Brodie Street Resource Library, Thunder Bay, this building has been successfully renovated, preserving the beauty of the original interior without compromising an efficient operation.*

Galt Carnegie library. *It was impossible to expand this building due to the constraints of the site, and it has been used for non-library purposes for many years.*

Renovations or additions which reflect concern for operating costs and the needs of senior or disabled citizens, and yet maintain the integrity of the original Carnegie design are still possible. Toronto is a good example. With seven of their branches originating as Carnegie libraries (either for Toronto or the earlier community of Toronto Junction) the Toronto Library Board embarked on a renewal programme in 1976. Typical of these are the Yorkville and Annette Branches, both of which have renovations and additions which complement the original, distinctive architecture while meeting changing library service requirements.

The Fort William—now Thunder Bay—Carnegie Library has also been restored close to its original condition, with architect, interior design consultant and librarian working together to achieve excellent results in historical, operational and aesthetic terms. The St. Thomas Carnegie building, although no longer serving a library function, is another example of a careful renovation, entirely sympathetic to the earlier design and concepts. The work done in renovating or restoring the Carnegie libraries in the American state of Ohio should also be mentioned. A recent survey of the 105 Carnegie libraries in that state revealed that seventy-six were still in use as libraries and that in many communities these buildings served both as tourist attractions and points of reference. The feeling of "being home, the sense of permanence, the fond recollection of childhood reading" have directed many Ohio communities to hold their Carnegie libraries in a place of near veneration, either maintaining them as libraries or re-cycling them for some other public purpose.[1]

The City of Cleveland, like Toronto with many Carnegie buildings among its 33 branches, has had an award winning renovation completed by David L. Holzheimer, Koster and Associates, Architects. This Cleveland firm has overcome access problems in this and other Carnegie renovations through the use of small, open elevators, and relies on modern lighting techniques to emphasize the beauty of the original building design, whether Modified Renaissance, French Renaissance, or a copy of the British building for the St. Louis Exposition (in turn copied from Christopher Wren's design for the Orangery at Kensington Palace).[2]

Other cities and towns in the United States are also recognizing the value of their Carnegie libraries. "Our Carnegie has been a focal point of civic pride through its life, and there is a strong community sentiment in favor of retaining the original character of the building," reported Brian Davis of the Iowa Public Library, in response to questions from the American Library Association. Residents of Watertown, Wisconsin passed a referendum which favoured retention of their Carnegie library, renovated, over a newer, more modern facility, and Cedar Rapids, Iowa citizens defeated four referenda that would have caused the Library to move from the Carnegie building to a new library. Also in Iowa, fifty-three Carnegie libraries have been moved to the National Register of Historic Places.[3]

The American consensus that preservation of Carnegie libraries is desirable in most instances is not matched in the United Kingdom. Although a few libraries have published jubilee histories expressing tribute and warm appreciation to Carnegie, the high cost of renovation to make the older buildings acceptable for new library services has placed the majority in disfavour.[4]

Influence

It is not difficult to understand why the Carnegie grants for library buildings were discontinued when one considers the frustration of those, particularly Bertram, dealing most intimately with them. The inability of many communities to complete their building within the granted amount, the ineptitude or unwillingness of architects to meet Bertram's concepts of "effective accommodation," the waste of money through increasing decoration, the broken pledges, the petty complaints and arguments—all have been documented. By the beginning of the first world war, therefore, the Carnegie Corporation was using questionnaires in the United States and the Inspector of Public Libraries in Ontario to determine the status of communities still requesting or already recipients of Carnegie benevolence. It was known by this time that at least some of the maintenance pledges were not being respected, and other abuses, such as the introduction of basement dance halls, were suspected of other communities.

In order to confirm their suspicions directly and to shape future policies about libraries and the grant programme, the Carnegie Corporation, in November, 1915, asked Alvin S. Johnson, an economics professor from Cornell University, to make a study or survey of the American Carnegie libraries. His report, which followed a ten week tour of the United States from east to west with visits to a hundred Carnegie libraries of varying size and character, was submitted to the Carnegie Corporation in 1916.[1] It was never officially published. Johnson's philosophy of both the purpose and methodology of what he called "library establishment" diverged so entirely from that of Bertram that it was impossible for the Corporation to adopt his Report's recommendations as long as Bertram remained Secretary.

Johnson summarized his views of the Carnegie building program in his autobiography, *Pioneer's Progress*:

> Andrew Carnegie had been more passionate about libraries than about anything else in his whole private life, and in his will he had made colossal provision for the building of libraries. Fifty millions had gone into the venture, and the corporation had never even inquired how the libraries were functioning. A community applied for a library: the corporation examined the figures for population and, according to the figures, made a grant of ten, fifteen, twenty-five, or fifty thousand, with the stipulation that the community should supply every year fifteen[2] per cent of the grant in maintenance. The service was administered by James Bertram, employee and friend of Andrew Carnegie, who after Carnegie's death made a sort of religion out of planting libraries. The only control he ever exercised was over the architectural plans, which he tried to have uniform from Bangor, Maine, to Calexico, California.[3]

In the report itself, Johnson first discussed the relationship of the free public library to social or public services, concluding that the library was an essential part of a system of advanced education. Moreover, he emphasized that business, industry, the professions and the trades, including agriculture, depended on access to the technical literature. However, he then questioned why philanthropist funds were necessary or should even be considered to relieve the local authorities from providing what was so essential a public service. While admitting that such funds

Preston Carnegie library. *Picture post cards were frequently used to express a community's pride in its Carnegie library.*

Carnegie Portrait engraved in crystal.

had been and would continue to be important in the less advanced states such as Alabama, or even in less sophisticated small communities in the better developed Eastern States, Johnson concluded that it was time to shift support, for the most part, from library buildings to library services. In this regard he felt that a key issue was library personnel, noting that a good building with a bad librarian was likely to represent waste of capital. He stated that he had not found one well-managed library without a trained librarian. In a separate section of the report Johnson dealt with the necessity for improvement in library education and training as well as an increase in facilities and scholarships, and recommended that Carnegie funds be channelled in this direction rather than to buildings.

In his discussion of the Carnegie buildings themselves Johnson did not hesitate in stating that the controls imposed by the Carnegie Corporation had resulted in the later buildings displaying remarkable adaption to the requirements of economy and efficiency. Noting that since those controls had gained the disapprobation of both architects and builders, he surmised that relaxation would lead to a return to the type of library building characterized by an imposing exterior, large halls of no value for library purposes, lecture rooms and galleries supposed in a vague way to reflect credit upon the town. He identified specific Carnegie libraries, such as that in Fort Worth, Texas, which were "half waste" as far as genuine library purposes were concerned. Unused rotundas (it would appear) were not limited to Sarnia or Brantford.

Johnson also suggested that the differing characteristics of a local community should be reflected in the distribution of floor space; one library might need a large children's area, while another might require a technical reference library. Flexibility in allowing the allocation of space to library functions was therefore of prime importance. He endorsed the concept of flexibility with respect to the combination of other community services in the library—the composite library to which Bertram had so ardently objected.

Another characteristic of the Carnegie libraries which Johnson identified as a problem in the United States was with the provision of a site. Advocating that a public library should be located on a major traffic route near the heart of the business or commercial district of the community, Johnson described some libraries which had been placed in locations where the average citizen simply would not venture. Worse, he stated, were some which people would go out of their way to avoid. He concluded that only ten per cent of the American Carnegie library sites were well chosen and regretted that more control had not been exerted over this circumstance.

Finally, Johnson pointed out that many of the Carnegie libraries had been neglected—in spite of the pledge of maintenance. Moreover, he argued that the ten per cent (of the total building cost) requested was inadequate, in the most part, to provide support as required. His summation of his recommendations, included in his autobiography, is very brief, as is his description of the inevitable confrontation with Bertram:

> First, I recommended the setting up, by the corporation, of a machinery for bringing in, every year, a detailed report of the operations of all existing Carnegie libraries.
> Second, no more libraries to be planted except after a thorough survey of the community, its sentiments, its needs, its realization of the importance of trained library service, and its willingness to pay for service.

Third, divert as much as practicable of available library funds to the promotion and support of library training.[4]

The confrontation followed, with Johnson describing how Bertram "swung his hatchet:"

> Your proposals, Doctor Johnson, fly straight in the face of Mr. Carnegie's intentions. He wanted to give libraries to communities and leave the communities absolutely free to manage them any way they might see fit. He abominated centralized, bureaucratic control. That is exactly what you want to introduce.
>
> Mr. Carnegie never wanted an unnecessary cent to be spent in the administration of his charities. I have administered the whole huge enterprise of establishing libraries with just one secretary, with a desk in my room. To do what you propose would require twelve secretaries and at least six rooms—a big unnecessary expense.

Johnson fought back: "Not so huge an expense, I ventured to say, for keeping track of an investment of fifty millions." "A big expense, and unnecessary," Mr. Bertram reiterated. "And as for library training, Mr. Carnegie never believed in it. He believed in having books where anybody could get hold of them. What made him, he used to say, was a private library a philanthropic gentleman opened to him. A librarian's business is to hand out the books. That doesn't require a long, expensive training."[5]

No further discussion was allowed at the meeting, and although the Board did move to terminate the building grants a year later, Johnson's Report was never accepted. It wasn't until the next decade (in the 1920's), with Bertram's influence less in evidence, that Johnson's recommendations about library education were implemented by the Carnegie Corporation, and funds were channelled to the establishment of library schools; to support of the American Library Association; and for library service demonstration projects of various kinds.

Many conclusions or recommendations similar to Johnson's are contained in the reports or letters of the Ontario Public Library Inspectors. T.W.H. Leavitt identified the importance of trained librarians as early as 1908, suggesting that Library Boards which neglected to become familiar with modern methodologies through the Library Institutes which made training available should have their provincial grants terminated. He described the new librarian as one who had ceased to be a mere custodian concerned with the purchase and preservation of musty volumes and who had become the head of a business undertaking. Leavitt also believed the public library to be crucial to the development of the community and the state, providing much more than a mere collection of books, but rather a combination of social and civilizing forces. He, like Johnson, felt that more grants, whether government or philanthropic, were not the answer for an increased awareness of the necessity of library service or for that service itself. He also preferred that the local community discover for itself the benefit of library service, and suggested that any government grants should be related to results, with impartial judges assisting in those assessments.

W.R. Nursey continued the emphasis on library training in his reports to the Minister of Education, including in a list of his 1909 duties, two items:

The direction of the attention of incompetents, (librarians) of which there are too many, to the only summer school in Canada as yet established for their special benefit, viz., the McGill Summer School for Librarians, in Montreal;

The devising of some plan for opening a similar school in the Province of Ontario.[6]

An analysis of the suitability of the Ontario Carnegie library sites or of the buildings themselves, similar to Johnson's, was not made by any of the Inspectors during the Carnegie grant period. However, descriptions of individual libraries included in their annual reports do contain specific comments about the buildings. Most severe is the 1906 critique of the Goderich Carnegie Library, which identified the following defects:

No provision made for increasing capacity of stack room;

In severe weather one furnace is not sufficient;

The building [plan] is defective; the librarian is not able to see into the reading rooms from the delivery desk.[7]

The Brockville Library was criticized because "The roof is a trifle too flat for the Canadian winter; and a door from the basement should have been provided."[8] Defects in the Lindsay Library were also noted:

The basement is too deep in the ground, giving the building a low appearance, as the site is flat, although slightly terraced immediately around the building.

The smoking room is not properly ventilated.

The reading room is not large enough to allow for the growth of the town. This may be overcome somewhat by throwing the present reading room, the main hall and children's room into one general room, extending the width of the building. While complete as at present, the plan does not seem to admit of further enlargement.

The heating apparatus was not of sufficient capacity. This has been partially remedied by the installation of extra radiators.[9]

It is of some interest that none of these Ontario critiques make mention of the wasteful rotundas or domes or of the over-generous lecture rooms about which the Johnson Report was so critical.

Johnson's criticism of the American library sites does not fully apply to the Ontario Carnegie libraries. As mentioned earlier, the Ontario libraries, almost without exception, were located in the heart of the town or village commercial and civic government area. In spite of changes which the past seven decades have brought to each community it is most common to find the Carnegie Library, next to the Town Hall or the Fire Station and near the local shops. Only the size of a few of the original sites, limited from expansion by a river (Galt), or too close to lot lines (Fort William and Hespeler) have created serious problems.

Whether or not the Ontario libraries were more successful in their arrangements or services than those in the United States did not influence either the Johnson report or the subsequent action of the Carnegie Corporation. The library building grant programme officially ended in November, 1917, with no new grants made after that time, either in the United States or the Commonwealth. Only those communities, such as Gravenhurst or Welland, where the gift process was already well underway, received their grants and completed their library buildings after 1917.

175

Evaluations of the Carnegie building grants and their impact on the development of public library services in the United States have been made periodically since the grants ended. In the thirties a European assessment of the American programme concluded that the Carnegie buildings had caused an increased understanding of the significance of public library service.[10] Somewhat later, an American librarian, Ralph Munn, disagreed, suggesting that "many millions of Americans have known only these small village and town Carnegie libraries and have formed their entire concept of the public library from them." He concluded that "These libraries, too small to provide even the minimum essentials of good service, have been in part responsible for the attitude of benevolent apathy with which so many people regard public libraries."[11]

The official view of the Carnegie Corporation is that the many small libraries scattered around the world created a generation of library users willing to vote for local or federal support for improved library services.[12] Carnegie library authority George Bobinski endorses this view in the American context:

> . . . Carnegie's philanthropy widened the acceptance of the principle of local government responsibility for the public library. The method of giving was not perfect. Poor sites were often selected. The ten per cent support pledge was sometimes broken or more often not surpassed. Nevertheless, it was a wise provision. It placed pressure on government bodies and the public to accept the organization and maintenance of the public library as a governmental service.[13]

Bobinski, in his study, *Carnegie Libraries*, also provides an assessment of the architecture of the buildings, dismissing derogatory comments as generally referring to the older buildings built before the Corporation and James Bertram had instituted controls. He feels that the architectural memorandum issued by Bertram in 1911 led to more open, flexible and less elaborate buildings and was the beginning of modern library architecture.[14]

An assessment of the Carnegie grant programme in the United Kingdom, similar to the Johnson study, was conducted shortly after responsibility for the library building programme there had been assigned to the Carnegie United Kingdom Trust. Dr. W.G.S. Adams, Professor of Political Theory and Institutions at Oxford, submitted a report to the Trust in 1914 after a six month evaluation of the United Kingdom library scene. He concluded that the grants had exercised a far reaching influence on the library movement, making possible in many centres a development which would not otherwise have come into existence. "The Carnegie grants have brought home the idea of the free public library as an important local institution," he stated. But he added: "The chief criticism concerns grants made to centres which have been unwilling or unable to support a library on the scale Mr. Carnegie provided. It may be summed up in the word 'overbuilding'."[15]

A similar analysis made in 1969 by James G. Olle suggests that the library support legislation in force in the United Kingdom at the time of the Carnegie grants was a great part of the problem, and that, on balance, money was saved for many communities through provision of a free building. He concluded that Carnegie and Bertram should not be blamed for the lack of distinction in architectural design, pointing out that they "tried to discourage extravagance in design and useless architectural features."[16]

Looking back on the two decades of Andrew Carnegie's library benefaction in Ontario, the criticisms frequently heard at the time, most often directed at the source of his wealth or the personal motivation for his philanthropy, have little relevance. More recent criticism usually relates to the inability of the smaller community to support an independent library. Experience has shown that it is increasingly more efficient for that small community to be served as part of a county or regional system. It could be argued that without their own Carnegie building some communities would have more willingly become part of such a network. The success of Carnegie libraries as branches of various Ontario County or Regional systems supports the view, however, that the buildings need not be hindrances to the coordination of library services.

Other current criticisms relate to Carnegie library plans and architecture. As discussed earlier, access problems caused by long flights of stairs, the necessity for supervision of two small floors rather than one larger one, and the inflexibility of the very early buildings with their separate rooms and delivery halls, have led to problems in adapting to modern building or library standards. The Toronto renovation initiative, among others, has demonstrated that these difficulties can be surmounted successfully. Hundreds of gifted librarians have used initiative and innovation to extend the service capabilities of the Ontario Carnegie libraries, and the incredible use that Bertram's "effective accommodation" encouraged in buildings, both monumental and modest, also attests to their success.

The free public library movement was firmly established in Ontario prior to the Carnegie grants. The Department of Education already provided incentives for library development and growth, for library education and training, and for resources. Inspector Leavitt pointed out in 1908 that the grants made for library purposes by the Ontario Legislature compared "more than favourably with those made by the most progressive State Legislations in the neighboring Republic."[17] As their initial response to the Carnegie Corporation indicated, all 105 of the Ontario communities (including Weston, Mimico and Toronto Junction) which received Carnegie grants already had libraries, either public or free public, prior to applying for a Carnegie building.

However, the reports and letters of the Public Library Inspectors reveal that the possibility of a free building acted as a catalyst in some communities for speeding the adoption by Council of the Public Libraries Act. In other communities, with the free public library already considered an essential element of local government, the Carnegie building provided a focus for increased support for library services. Rivalry to secure a Carnegie Library among neighbouring communities or within a county, as has been demonstrated, heightened the awareness of library development, particularly in rural Ontario. The publicity—and in some instances controversy—which surrounded each step of the grant seeking, site selection and plan approval process, also helped to spread the message of Andrew Carnegie's dramatic philanthropy. A debt of gratitude is owed to him and to the Carnegie Corporation: the present Ontario library scene, without the impetus which the library building programme created, would not be as positive. For many, many thousands of users, whether in an urban environment or travelling from the farm for Saturday shopping, the libraries represented—and continue to provide—education, opportunity and adventure, a necessary stability and permanence. The Carnegie Library *was* "the best gift," and it is a heritage that must not be lost.

Woodstock Carnegie library. *This building epitomizes the grace and dignity of the Ontario Carnegie libraries, and is an ever present reminder of the value of Andrew Carnegie's gifts to this province.*

Appendix 1

List of Ontario Carnegie Library Grants by Date

Date	Community	Population At Grant Promise Time	Total Grant $	Per Capita Grant $
1901				
Feb 13	Windsor	11,000	27,000	2.45
Aug 16	Collingwood	6,000	14,500	2.41
Oct 17	Guelph	11,496	24,000	2.08
Nov 6	Ottawa	58,000	100,000	1.72
Dec 14	Sault Ste. Marie	7,000	15,500	2.21
Dec 14	Stratford	11,000	15,000	1.36
Dec 21	Cornwall	7,000	8,000	1.14
Dec 31	St. Catharines	9,946	25,000	2.51
1902				
Jan 10	Sarnia	8,000	20,000	2.50
Jan 23	Smiths Falls	5,600	11,000	1.96
Jan 23	Lindsay	7,000	13,500	1.92
Feb 4	Palmerston	2,000	10,000	5.00
Feb 13	Chatham	9,068	19,000	2.09
Mar 14	Goderich	4,185	10,000	2.38
Mar 14	Berlin	9,747	40,900	4.19
Apr 11	Brampton	2,950	12,500	4.23
Apr 11	Brantford	17,000	48,000	2.82
Apr 11	Galt	8,100	23,000	2.83
Apr 26	Thorold	2,400	10,000	4.18
Jul 18	Waterloo	3,574	10,000	2.79
1903				
Jan 2	Paris	3,500	10,000	2.85
Jan 23	Toronto			
	Central Reference	181,000	275,000	2.20
	Yorkville Branch	NA	25,000	NA
	Queen & Lisgar Branch	NA	25,000	NA
	Riverdale Branch	NA	25,000	NA
Mar 20	St. Thomas	12,000	27,000	2.25
Apr 13	Brockville	9,000	17,500	1.94
Nov 25	Listowel	2,980	10,000	3.35
1904				
Mar 8	St. Marys	3,500	10,000	2.85
Jun 2	Owen Sound	9,479	25,000	2.63
Jun 2	Orangeville	3,700	12,500	3.37
Dec 30	Dundas	4,500	12,000	2.66

1905

Apr 20	Lucknow	1,111	7,500	6.75
Jul 6	Woodstock	10,000	24,000	2.40
Dec 8	Niagara Falls	4,244	15,000	3.53

1906

Feb 13	Picton	3,698	12,500	3.38
Feb 13	Perth	3,588	10,000	2.78
Mar 24	Wallaceburg	3,500	11,500	3.28
Mar 24	Gravenhurst	1,621	7,000	4.31
Mar 24	Bracebridge	3,000	10,000	3.33
Apr 10	Kincardine	2,700	5,000	1.85
Apr 23	Kemptville	1,600	3,000	1.87
May 15	Hanover	2.500	10,000	4.00
Nov 24	Oshawa	4,394	14,000	3.18
Nov 27	Dresden	1,475	8,000	5.42

1907

Mar 9	Port Elgin	1,600	8,800	5.55
Apr 8	Teeswater	930	10,000	10.75
Dec 13	Penetanguishene	2,422	13,000	5.36
Dec 24	Pembroke	5,624	14,000	2.48

1908

Jan 29	Fergus	1,600	7,000	4.37
Mar 21	Mitchell	2,000	6,000	3.00
Mar 21	Peterborough	11,739	30,000	2.55
Apr 6	Toronto Junction	NA	20,000	NA
May 8	Harriston	2,000	10,000	5.00
Jun 29	Ingersoll	5,000	10,000	2.00
Jul 20	Seaforth	2,267	10,000	4.41
Aug 8	Toronto			
	Wychwood Branch	NA	20,000	NA
	High Park Branch	NA	15,000	NA
	Beaches Branch	NA	15,000	NA
Nov 20	Fort William	9,000	50,000	5.55
Dec 24	Milverton	1,025	7,000	6.82

1909

Feb 13	Preston	3,500	12,000	3.42
Feb 13	Grand Valley	1,000	7,500	7.50
Mar 13	Brussels	1,400	7,000	5.00
Mar 23	Elora	1,500	6,400	4.26
Mar 23	Hamilton	60,000	100,000	1.66
Apr 10	Mount Forest	2,019	10,000	4.95
Apr 10	Orillia	4,907	13,500	2.75
Dec 24	Ayr	807	5,200	6.44

1910

Jan 18	Hespeler	2,522	14,280	5.66
Jan 31	Simcoe	3,425	10,000	2.91
Mar 21	Leamington	2,451	10,000	4.07
Mar 21	Midland	4,500	12,500	2.77
Apr 16	New Liskeard	3,000	10,900	3.63
Apr 28	Beaverton	1,100	7,000	6.36

1911

Jan 6	Campbellford	2,485	8,000	3.21
Jan 6	Durham	2,000	8,000	4.00
Jan 6	Essex	1,353	6,000	4.43
Jan 6	Grimsby	1,500	8,000	5.33
Jan 6	Markdale	1,015	7,000	6.89
Jan 6	Port Hope	5,000	10,000	2.00
Jan 21	Shelburne	1,200	6,000	5.00
Mar 18	Elmira	1,060	7,000	6.60
Mar 29	Kingsville	1,750	5,000	2.85
Mar 29	Walkerton	3,090	10,000	3.25

Apr 8	Amherstburg	3,000	10,000	3.33
Apr 8	Whitby	2,500	10,000	4.00
Apr 25	North Bay	7,815	16,395	2.09
May 16	Forest	1,553	5,000	3.21
Nov 21	Aylmer	2,049	8,000	3.90

1912

| Apr 30 | New Hamburg | 1,485 | 8,000 | 5.39 |
| May 17 | Watford | 1,105 | 6,000 | 5.42 |

1913

Jan 2	Exeter	1,554	8,000	5.14
Jan 2	Tillsonburg	2,850	10,000	3.50
Jan 2	Weston	2,000	10,000	5.00
Apr 28	Stouffville	1,025	5,000	4.87
May 21	Kenora	6,159	15,000	2.43
Dec 8	Welland	5,311	25,000	4.70

1914

Jan 14	Parkhill	1,289	8,000	6.20
Feb 26	Mimico	1,373	7,500	5.46
Apr 13	Stirling	848	5,000	5.89
Apr 13	Tavistock	1,028	7,500	7.29
May 8	Norwich	1,024	7,000	5.81
May 8	Fort Francis	3,000	10,000	3.33
Jun 11	Norwood	888	5,000	5.63
Jul 23	Barrie	6,420	15,000	2.33
Nov 11	Glencoe	950	5,000	5.26

1915

| Jan 6 | Clinton (addition only) | 2,251 | 4,900 | 2.17 |
| Mar 16 | Renfrew | 4,000 | 16,000 | 4.06 |

1916

| Mar 31 | Merritton | 1,670 | 8,500 | 5.08 |

1917

| Mar 31 | Ottawa (West Branch) | NA | 15,000 | NA |

Appendix 2

Expanded List or Schedule of Questions
Free Public Library

1. Town? _____

2. Population? _____

3. Has it a Library at present? _____

4. Number of Books (excluding Government Reports)? _____

5. Circulation for past year? _____

6. How is Library housed? _____

7. Number and measurements of Rooms, and their uses? _____
_____

8.   Finances according to last Yearly Report

Receipts:		Expenditures:	
City Appropriation	$ _____	Rent	$ _____
Bequests	_____	Salaries	_____
Miscellaneous Receipts	_____	Books	_____
_____	_____	Miscellaneous	_____
Total Revenue for year $ _____		Total Expenditures $ _____	

9. Rate and Amount which Councils will pledge for support of Library yearly (levying tax for purpose) if Building obtained? _____
_____

10. Is requisite site available? _____

11. Amount now Collected toward Building? _____

To facilitate Mr. Carnegie's consideration of your appeal, will you oblige by filling in the above, and returning with statement of any other particulars likely to assist in making decision.

This blank is sent for the purpose of summarizing information and does not imply favorable consideration of the appeal.

It is necessary to give explicit answer to each question, as in the absence of such, there is no basis for action, and the matter will be delayed pending further communication.

Respectfully,

Signature _____   J.A.S. BERTRAM, Secretary,
                                                          8 East 91st Street,
Designation _____   New York

Appendix 3

A Resolution
To accept the donation of Andrew Carnegie

WHEREAS, Andrew Carnegie has agreed to furnish _____ Dollars to the Corporation _____ to erect a FREE PUBLIC LIBRARY BUILDING, on condition that said Corporation — shall pledge itself by RESOLUTION OF COUNCIL, to support a FREE PUBLIC LIBRARY, at cost of not less than _____ a year, and PROVIDE A SUITABLE SITE for said building: now therefore

BE IT RESOLVED by the Council of the Corporation of the town of _____ that said Corporation accept said DONATION, and it does hereby pledge itself to comply with the requirements of said ANDREW CARNEGIE.

RESOLVED, that it will furnish a suitable SITE for said BUILDING, and will maintain a FREE PUBLIC LIBRARY in said BUILDING when erected, at a cost of not less than _____ Dollars a year.

RESOLVED, that an ANNUAL LEVY shall hereafter be made upon the taxable property of said Corporation sufficient in amount to comply with the above requirements.

CLERK   Mayor

I, Clerk of the Corporation of _____ do hereby certify that the foregoing is a full and complete copy and transcript of a RESOLUTION passed by the COUNCIL of said Corporation at their regular session on the _____.

Witness my hand and the seal of said Corporation this _____ day of _____ 19____.

CLERK

Appendix 4

Carnegie Library Architects Identified*

Community	Architects
Amherstburg	C. Howard Crane
Aylmer	W.A. Mahoney
Ayr	W.E. Binning
Barrie	Chapman & McGiffin
Beaverton	W.E. Binning
Berlin	Chas. Knechtel
	— J.J. Beck (addition)
Bracebridge	G.M. Miller
Brampton	Wickson & Gregg
Brantford	Stewart, Stewart & Taylor
	— L.D. Barker (addition)
Brockville	B. Dillon
Brussels	Mr. Ireland
Campbellford	W.A. Mahoney
Chatham	T.J. Wilson
Clinton	J. Ades Fowler
Collingwood	W. & W. Stewart
Dundas	Chapman & McGiffin
Durham	W.A. Mahoney
Elmira	W.A. Mahoney
Elora	W.F. Sheppard
Essex	J.C. Pennington
Exeter	W.A. Mahoney
Fergus	W.A. Mahoney
Forest	W.A. Mahoney
Fort Frances	W.A. Mahoney
Fort William	Hood & Scott
Galt	Fred Mellish
Grand Valley	George Gray
Grimsby	A.E. Nicholson
Guelph	W. Frye Colwill
Hamilton	A.W. Peene
Hanover	W.E. Binning
Harriston	W.E. Binning
Hespeler	A.H. Crocker
Kemptville	A.S. Allaster
Kenora	John Manuel
Kincardine	J.W. Drake
Kingsville	J.C. Pennington
Leamington	Alex Maycock
Listowel	W.E. Binning

Lucknow	Beaumont Jarvis
Merritton	A.E. Nicholson
Milverton	J.A. Russell
Mimico	S. Coon & Son
Mitchell	W.E. Binning
Mount Forest	George Gray
New Hamburg	James A. Russell
New Liskeard	Angus & Angus
North Bay	Angus & Angus
Norwich	Edward Pollock
Orangeville	Beaumont Jarvis
Orillia	Mr. Crocker
Oshawa	Carrerre & Hastings
Ottawa	E.L. Horwood
Owen Sound	Finlay, Forster & Clark
Palmerston	W. Frye Colwill
Parkhill	W.A. Mahoney
Pembroke	Francis Sullivan
Penetanguishene	Charles P. Baird
Picton	Anglin, Peden & McLaren
Port Elgin	S.G. Kingsey
Port Hope	W.A. Mahoney
Preston	W.E. Binning
Renfrew	Mr. Millson
St. Catharines	Sydney R. Badgley
St. Marys	J.A. Humphris
Sarnia	M.R. Burrowes
Sault Ste. Marie	H. Russell Halton
	— Demar & Murdoch
	(2d building)
Seaforth	John Finlayson
Shelburne	J.A. McKennzie
Simcoe	Sheppard & Calvin
Smiths Falls	G.M. Bayley
Stirling	W.A. Mahoney
Stouffville	F.F. Saunders
Stratford	James A. Russell
Teeswater	W.E. Binning
Thorold	A.E. Nicholson
Tillsonburg	W.A. Mahoney
Toronto — Central Reference	Wickson & Gregg, A.H. Chapman
Wychwood Branch	Eden Smith
High Park Branch	Eden Smith
Beaches Branch	Eden Smith
Walkerton	George Gray
Wallaceburg	A.M. Piper
Watford	W.A. Mahoney
Welland	Norman Kearns
Weston	Lindsay & Brydon
Whitby	W.A. Mahoney
Windsor	John Scott & Co.
Woodstock	Chadwick & Beckett

*The architects listed have been identified through the Carnegie Library Correspondence files.

Notes

References are grouped by chapter or chapter section. In citing the Carnegie Library Correspondence (C.L.C.) the following conventions have been used:

C.L.C., Name of community, Microfilm reel no.,
e.g. C.L.C., Kenora, reel no. 15

When references are to letters or library board minutes held in the community or library archives, the citations are as follows:

Name of community, Library board minutes, date

In order to avoid confusion between the text and the correspondence which has been quoted, place names as they existed during the grant period have been used:

Berlin for Kitchener
Fort William for Thunder Bay
Galt ⎤
Hespeler ⎬ for Cambridge
Preston ⎦

Preface
1. George S. Bobinski, *Carnegie libraries: their history and impact on American public library development* (Chicago: American Library Association, 1969), p. viii.
2. Carnegie Corporation of New York, "List of library bildings in United States, Canada, United Kingdom and other English-Speaking countries" (1913: Revised to 1915).
3. Durand R. Miller, comp. *Carnegie grants for library buildings, 1890-1917.* (New York: Carnegie Corp., 1943).

Introduction
1. Andrew Carnegie, "Wealth," *North American Review*, CXLVIII (June, 1889), 653-654; reprinted in Edward C. Kirkland, ed., *The Gospel of Wealth and Other Timely Essays* (Cambridge, Mass.: Harvard University Press, 1962).
2. Andrew Carnegie, "The best fields for philanthropy, *North American Review*, CXLIX (December 1889), 688-689; reprinted in above.
3. Christopher Neale, "The first Carnegie free library," Unpublished essay (Dunfermline, 1976).
4. Joseph Frazier Wall, *Andrew Carnegie*, (New York: Oxford University Press, 1970), pp. 107-108.
5. *Ibid.*
6. *Ibid.*
7. Miller, *op. cit.* p. 8.
8. The Carnegie Corporation does not include the grant to the library in Nairobi, Kenya, as a building grant. The records of that library indicate that a grant made for other purposes was in fact used for the building, at least in part, and the library is popularly known as the McMillan-Carnegie Library.
9. Robert Lester, *Review of grants for library interests, 1911-1935* (New York: Carnegie Corp., 1935), pp. 149-150.
10. Miller, *op. cit.* p. 8

Chapter 1
1. Eric Bow, "The public library movement in nineteenth century Ontario," *Ontario Library Review*, LXVI (1982), p. 2
2. *Ibid.*, p. 3.
3. *Ibid.*
4. Ontario, Department of Education, *Report of the Minister* (1910), p. 485.
5. 14 & 15 Victoria, Chapter 86, *Provincial Statutes of Canada* (1851).
6. Ontario, Department of Education, *op. cit.*, (1910), p. 485.
7. Bow, *op. cit.*, p. 4.
8. Bow, *op. cit.*, p. 5.
9. 13 & 14 Victoria, Chapter 48, *Provincial Statutes of Canada* (1850).

10. Bow, *op. cit.*, pp. 9-10.
11. *Ibid.*
12. Lorne Bruce, "Public library policies in Ontario, 1882-1920," Unpublished report, Guelph, Ontario, pp. 5-12.
13. 45 Victoria, Chapter 22, *Revised Statutes of Ontario* (1882).
14. 58 Victoria, Chapter 45, *Revised Statutes of Ontario* (1895).
15. Ontario, Department of Education, *op. cit.* (1910), p. 486.
16. Bow, *op. cit.*, p. 17.

Chapter 2

The grant programme
1. Frank Pierce Hill, *James Bertram: an Appreciation*, (New York: Carnegie Corp., 1936), pp. 19-25.
2. *Ibid.*, p. 28.
3. *Ibid.*, p. 32.
4. *Ibid.*
5. Wall, *op. cit.*, pp. 891-892.
6. Hill, *op. cit.*, p. 34.
7. Bobinski, *op. cit.*, p. 31.
8. C.L.C., Hanover, reel no. 13.
9. Hill, *op. cit.*, p. 34.
10. *Ibid.*, p. 62.

1901: the first Ontario grants
1. Miller, *op. cit.*, 40 p.
2. C.L.C., Collingwood, reel no. 6.
3. C.L.C., Windsor, reel no. 34.
4. *Ibid.*
5. Windsor, Library Board minutes, February 1902. Undated clipping from *The Evening Record*, included in the Minutes.
6. C.L.C., Windsor, reel no. 34.
7. Ontario, Department of Education, *op. cit.* (1906), pp. 187-319.
8. C.L.C., Collingwood, reel no. 6.
9. *Ibid.*
10. C.L.C., Guelph, reel no. 13.
11. *Ibid.*
12. *Ibid.*
13. C.L.C., Ottawa, reel no. 23.
14. J. Castell Hopkins, ed., *Canadian annual review of public affairs, 1906* (Toronto: Annual Review Pub. Co., 1907), pp. 628-629.
15. C.L.C., Ottawa, reel no. 23.
16. C.L.C., Sault Ste. Marie, reel no. 28.
17. *Ibid.*
18. *Ibid.*
19. *Ibid.*
20. A.W. Fisher, "Statford; centenary of the public library," Unpublished history (1946), p. 4.
21. C.L.C., Stratford, reel no. 30.
22. *Ibid.*
23. *Ibid.* It is of interest to note that Barnett's library interests were more extensive than his work on behalf of the Stratford Library Board. He was a noted bibliophile, and donated his 40,000 volume personal library to the University of Western Ontario in 1918.
24. C.L.C., Cornwall, reel no. 7.
25. *Ibid.*
26. C.L.C., St. Catharines, reel no. 27.
27. *Ibid.*
28. *Ibid.*
29. *Ibid.*
30. *Ibid.* Undated clipping from unidentified newspaper in the St. Catharines correspondence file.

Procedures, problems and opposition
1. C.L.C., St. Thomas reel no. 27.
2. C.L.C., Grand Valley, reel no. 12.
3. C.L.C., Ayr, reel no. 2.
4. C.L.C., Forest, reel no. 10.
5. C.L.C., Hamilton, reel no. 13.
6. *Ibid.*
7. *Ibid.*
8. *Ibid.*
9. C.L.C., Brussels, reel no. 4.
10. C.L.C., St. Marys, reel no. 27.
11. C.L.C., Grand Valley, reel no. 12.
12. Alan Ironside, "The Orillia Library," *Anecdotes of Old Orillia* (Orillia Historical Society, 1977-78).
13. *Ibid.*
14. C.L.C., Orillia, reel no. 23.
15. C.L.C., Midland, reel no. 19.
16. *Ibid.*
17. C.L.C. Guelph, reel no. 13. Undated clipping in Guelph correspondence file.
18. Bobinski, *op. cit.*, p. 104.
19. C.L.C., Walkerton, reel no. 33.
20. C.L.C., Wallaceburg, reel no. 33.
21. C.L.C., Grand Valley, reel no 12.
22. *Ibid.*
23. C.L.C., Palmerston, reel no. 24.
24. C.L.C., Lucknow, reel no. 18.
25. *Ibid.*
26. C.L.C., Hanover, reel no. 13.
27. *Ibid.*
28. C.L.C., Harriston, reel no. 13.

Grants and pledges
1. C.L.C., reel nos. 1-35.
2. *Ibid.*
3. C.L.C., Teeswater, reel no. 31. Note the address.
4. *Ibid.*
5. *Ibid.*
6. C.L.C., Kitchener (Berlin), reel no. 15.
7. *Ibid.*
8. *Ibid.*
9. *Ibid.*
10. *Ibid.*
11. *Ibid.*
12. C.L.C., reel nos. 1-35.
13. Ontario, Department of Education, *op. cit.* (1909), pp. 405-406.
14. C.L.C., Tilbury, reel no. 31.
15. C.L.C., St. Thomas, reel no. 27.
16. Ontario, Department of Education, *op. cit.* (1906), p. 233.
17. London Public Library Board minutes, February 6, 1913.
18. *Ibid.*, December 13, 1978.
19. Simcoe Public Library, Archives, Undated letter.
20. Fergus Public Library Board minutes, June 1, 1909.
21. C.L.C., Tavistock, reel no. 31.
22. C.L.C., Tillsonburg, reel no. 31.
23. C.L.C., Dresden, reel no. 8.
24. *Ibid.*
25. C.L.C., Hanover, reel no. 13.
26. *Ibid.*
27. *Ibid.*
28. C.L.C., Harriston, reel no. 13
29. C.L.C., Grand Valley, reel no. 12.

Carnegie, Bertram and the inspectors of Public Libraries
1. *The Citizen*, Ottawa (April 30, 1906).
2. *Ibid.*
3. *The Saturday Evening Citizen*, Ottawa (April 28, 1906).
4. *The Citizen*, Ottawa (April 30, 1906).
5. *Ibid.*
6. *The Citizen*, Ottawa (May 1, 1906).
7. *Ibid.*

8. *The Citizen*, Ottawa (April 30, 1906).
9. *The Citizen*, Ottawa (May 1, 1906).
10. *The Globe*, Toronto (April 28, 1906).
11. *Ibid.*
12. Miller, *op. cit.*, p. 40
13. *The Globe*, Toronto (April 28, 1906).
14. *Ibid.*
15. C.L.C., Smiths Falls, reel no. 30.
16. *Ibid.*
17. Smiths Falls Public Library Board minutes, May, 1906.
18. C.L.C., St. Catharines, reel no. 27.
19. C.L.C., Wallaceburg, reel no. 33.
20. C.L.C., Forest, reel no. 10.
21. *Ibid.*
22. C.L.C., Picton, reel no. 25.
23. C.L.C., Hamilton, reel no. 13.
24. Skibo Estate, Sutherland, Scotland. Catalogue of Sale (1982).
25. C.L.C., Picton, reel no. 25.
26. C.L.C., Guelph, reel no. 13.
27. C.L.C., Kitchener (Berlin), reel no. 15.
28. C.L.C., Hamilton, reel no. 13.
29. C.L.C., Tavistock, reel no. 31 (Clipping included in file).
30. Hill, *op. cit.*, p. 67.
31. C.L.C., Hanover, reel no. 13.
32. C.L.C., Ingersoll, reel no. 15.
33. C.L.C., Penetanguishene, reel no. 24.
34. *Ibid.*
35. C.L.C., Ingersoll, reel no. 15
36. C.L.C., Exeter, reel no. 10.
37. C.L.C., Thorold, reel no. 31.
38. C.L.C., Kenora, reel no. 15.
39. *Ibid.*
40. C.L.C., Stouffville, reel no. 30.
41. C.L.C., Waterloo, reel no. 33.
42. C.L.C., St. Marys, reel no. 27.
43. C.L.C., Clinton, reel no. 6.
44. Ontario, Department of Education, *op. cit.* (1906), p. 222.
45. *Ibid.*, p. 224.
46. *Ibid.*, pp. 224-319.
47. *Ibid.* (1937), p. 289.
48. C.L.C., New Liskeard, reel no. 21.
49. C.L.C., Orillia, reel no. 23.
50. *Ibid.*
51. C.L.C., Elora, reel no. 9.
52. C.L.C., Orangeville, reel no. 23.
53. C.L.C., Thorold, reel no. 31.
54. C.L.C., Picton, reel no. 25.
55. C.L.C., Brampton, reel no. 4.
56. Ontario Department of Education, *op. cit.* (1908), p. 149.
57. *Ibid.* (1909), pp. 333-334.
58. *Ibid.* (1910), p. 450.
59. C.L.C., Campbellford, reel no. 5.
60. C.L.C., Waterloo, reel no. 33.
61. C.L.C., Markdale, reel no. 19. Undated clipping in the Markdale file.
62. C.L.C., Norwood, reel no. 22.
63. C.L.C., Kitchener (Berlin), reel no. 15.
64. C.L.C., Renfrew, reel no. 26.
65. C.L.C., Tavistock, reel no. 31.
66. C.L.C., Gravenhurst, reel no. 12.
67. *Ibid.* Note that Bertram ceased to use simplified spelling after Carnegie's death in 1919.
68. C.L.C., Stouffville, reel no. 30.
69. C.L.C., Welland, reel no. 34.

Toronto and its Branches
1. C.L.C., Toronto, reel no. 32.
2. *Ibid.* Undated clipping from *The Globe* (February, 1903), included in Toronto correspondence file.
3. *Ibid.*
4. *Ibid.*

5. *Ibid.*
6. Ontario, Department of Education, *op. cit.* (1906), p. 233.
7. *Ibid.*
8. *The Journal of the Royal Architectural Institute of Canada.* XXVII no. 2 (February, 1950), p. 74.
9. Ontario, Department of Education, *op. cit.* (1906), pp. 233-242.
10. C.L.C., Toronto, reel no. 32.
11. *Ibid.*
12. C.L.C., Toronto Junction, reel no. 32.
13. C.L.C., Toronto, reel no. 32.
14. *Ibid.*
15. *Ibid.*
16. *Ibid.*
17. *Ibid.*
18. *Ibid.*

Chapter 3

Plans and sites
1. George H. Locke, "Some warnings in regard to planning libraries." *The Journal of The Royal Architectural Institute of Canada*, III (May-June, 1926).
2. C.L.C., Brussels, reel no. 4. Note that the spelling of building in this letter is not in the simplified form which Bertram used at this date.
3. New York architects Edward Tilton and Henry Whitfield were frequently consulted by Bertram for advice or library layouts. (See Sandra J. Bolek, "Carnegie Libraries in Ohio." Draft of a history of the Carnegie libraries of Ohio, Cleveland, Ohio, 1982.)
4. C.L.C., Grand Valley, reel no. 12.
5. *Ibid.*
6. C.L.C., Thorold, reel no. 31.
7. C.L.C., Harriston, reel no. 13.
8. C.L.C., Forest, reel no. 10.
9. Locke, *op. cit.*
10. C.L.C. Shelburne, reel no. 29.
11. *Ibid.*
12. C.L.C., Barrie, reel no. 2. Note that Chapman at this date was associated with the firm of Chapman & McGiffen Architects, Toronto.
13. C.L.C., Hespeler, reel no. 14.
14. C.L.C., Brantford, reel no. 4.
15. C.L.C., Sarnia, reel no. 28.
16. Ontario, Department of Education, *op. cit.* (1906), pp. 276-279.
17. There were several editions of "Notes on Library Bildings," with little difference in the information presented. The title varied: "Notes on the Erection of Library Buildings" was the title on the edition sent to many Ontario Library Boards.
18. It is interesting to note that this is the same percentage for the identical period of Carnegie library construction in the United States.
19. "Notes on Library Bildings." (New York: Carnegie Corporation, 1911).
20. *Ibid.*
21. C.L.C., Barrie, reel no. 2.
22. C.L.C., Exeter, reel no. 10.
23. C.L.C., Kemptville, reel no. 15.
24. C.L.C., Grand Valley, reel no. 12.
25. C.L.C., Hespeler, reel no. 14.
26. George H. Locke, "The Toronto Public Libraries." *The Journal of The Royal Architectural Institute of Canada*, III (May-June, 1926).

Design
1. Phyllis Lambert, "Notes on libraries: development of form and use." Unpublished report (1981).
2. Alan Gowans, *Building Canada: an Architectural History of Canadian Life* (Toronto: Oxford University Press, 1966).

3. Douglas Richardson, "A blessed sense of civic excess: the architecture of Union Station." *The Open Gate: Toronto Union Station*, ed. Richard Bebout (Toronto: Peter Martin Associates, 1972).
4. Marcus Whiffen, *American Architecture, 1607-1976* (Cambridge, Mass.: MIT Press, 1981).
5. Locke, "The Toronto Public Libraries," *op. cit.*, p. 87.
6. C.L.C., Toronto, reel no. 32.
7. *Ibid.*
8. C.L.C., Hanover, reel no. 13.
9. C.L.C., Harriston, reel no. 13. A later letter mentions that Binning had gone to Western Canada, and Bertram was asked if Forster and Clarke of Owen Sound could supervise the construction.
10. *Ibid.*
11. *Ibid.*
12. C.L.C., Durham, reel no. 9.
13. C.L.C., Stouffville, reel no. 30.
14. Martin Birkhaus, "Francis Sullivan, Architect." *The Journal of the Royal Architectural Institute of Canada*, XXXIX (March, 1962).
15. *Ibid.*, p. 34.
16. *Ibid.*, p. 32.
17. *Ibid.*
18. *Ibid.*

Architects
1. C.L.C., Barrie, reel no. 2.
2. C.L.C., Grimsby, reel no. 13.
3. C.L.C., Welland, reel no. 34.
4. C.L.C., Elora, reel no. 9.
5. *Ibid.*
6. C.L.C., Smiths Falls, reel no. 29.
7. C.L.C., Beaverton, reel no. 3.
8. *Ibid.*
9. C.L.C., Pembroke, reel no. 24.
10. *Ibid.*
11. *Ibid.*
12. *Ibid.*
13. *Ibid.*
14. Birkhaus, *op. cit.*, 32.
15. C.L.C., Pembroke, reel no. 24.
16. C.L.C., Shelburne, reel no. 29.
17. *Ibid.*
18. George H. Locke, "How Library ideals affect library architecture." *The Journal of The Royal Architectural Institute of Canada*, III (May-June, 1926), pp. 89-91.
19. *Ibid.*, pp. 90-91.

Construction and costs
1. Windsor Public Library, Archives. Undated clipping.
2. Kitchener Public Library, Archives. Copy of the original specification documents.
3. C.L.C., Guelph, reel no. 13.
4. Ontario, Department of Education, *op. cit.* (1906), pp. 276-279.
5. C.L.C., Collingwood, reel no. 6.
6. C.L.C., St. Marys, reel no. 27.

Chapter 4

Where they are — and were
1. C.L.C., Windsor, reel no. 34.
2. C.L.C., Hanover, reel no. 13.
3. Ontario, Department of Education, *op. cit.* (1906), p. 311.
4. *Ibid.*, p. 300. The Cutter table was a scheme designed by Charles Amni Cutter in 1891 for placing alphabetic entries in numerical sequence. With some modifications this scheme is still in use in today's libraries.
5. *Ibid.*, p. 306.
6. *Ibid.*, p. 270.
7. *Ibid.*, p. 295.

8. Ontario, Department of Education, *op. cit.* (1909), p. 417.
9. Ontario, Department of Education, *op. cit.* (1906), p. 295.
10. *Ibid.*, p. 304.
11. *Ibid.*, pp. 202-205.
12. Bruce, *op. cit.*, p. 30.
13. Ontario, Department of Education, *op. cit.*, (1906), p. 215.
14. *Ibid.*, p. 217.
15. *Ibid.*, p. 215.
16. Ontario, Department of Education, *op. cit.* (1909), p. 334.
17. Bruce, *op. cit.*, p. 30.
18. Ontario, Department of Education, *op. cit.* (1912), p. 545.

Renovations
1. Sandra J. Bolek, *op. cit.*, p. 5.
2. *Ibid.*, p. 9.
3. Susan Spaeth Cherry, "Carnegies Live: but the Destiny of a Beloved Institution is unfolding in Mixed Triumph and Tragedy," *American libraries*, XII (April 1981), pp. 184-188, 218-222.
4. J.G.H. Olle, "Andrew Carnegie: the Unloved Benefactor," *The Library World*, LXX (April 1969), pp. 255-262.

Influence
1. Alvin S. Johnson, *A Report to Carnegie Corporation of New York on the Policy of Donations to Free Public Libraries* (New York: Carnegie Corp., 1919). Although copies are available, this report was never officially published.
2. Note that fifteen per cent is in error: the Carnegie Corporation requirement for annual maintenance was ten per cent of the grant amount.
3. Alvin S. Johnson, *Pioneer's Progress: an Autobiography*. (New York: Viking Press, 1962), p. 235.
4. Johnson, *Pioneer's progress*, p. 238.
5. *Ibid.*
6. Ontario, Department of Education, *op. cit.* (1909), p. 334.
7. Ontario, Department of Education, *op. cit.* (1906), p. 226.
8. *Ibid.*, p. 252.
9. *Ibid.*, p. 276.
10. William Munthe, *American Librarianship from a European Angle: an Attempt at an Evaluation of Policies and Activities* (Chicago: American Library Association, 1939), p. 18.
11. Ralph Munn, "Hindsight on the gifts of Carnegie," *Library Journal*, LXXVI (December, 1951), p. 1966-1970.
12. Norman Horrocks, *The Carnegie Corporation of New York and its Impact on Library Development in Australia: a Case-study of Foundation Influence* (Unpublished Ph.D. Thesis, University of Pittsburgh, 1971), p. 60.
13. Bobinski, *op. cit.*, pp. 191-192.
14. *Ibid.*, p. 192.
15. Olle, *op. cit.*, p. 258.
16. *Ibid.*, p. 261.
17. Ontario, Department of Education, *op. cit.* (1908), p. 151.

Selected bibliography

Books

Bloomfield, Elizabeth and Gerald with Peter McCaskell. *Urban Growth and Local Services: the Development of Ontario Municipalities to 1981*. Guelph: University of Guelph, 1983.

Bobinski, George S. *Carnegie Libraries: their History and Impact on American Pubic Library Development*. Chicago: American Library Association, 1969.

Carnegie, Andrew. *Autobiography of Andrew Carnegie*. Boston: Houghton, Mifflin and Co., 1920.

Carnegie, Andrew. *The Gospel of Wealth and Other Timely Essays*. Edited by Edward C. Kirkland. Cambridge, Mass.: Harvard University Press, 1962.

Carnegie Endowment for International peace. *A Manual of the Public Benefactions of Andrew Carnegie*. Washington, D.C.: Carnegie Endowment for International Peace, 1919.

Champneys, Amion, L. *Public Libraries: a Treatise on their Design, Construction and Fittings*. London: Botsford, 1907.

Drexler, Arthur, ed. *The Architecture of the Ecole des Beaux Arts*. New York: Museum of Modern Art, 1977.

Gowans, Alan. *Building Canada: an Architectural History of Canadian Life*. Toronto: Oxford University Press, 1966.

Hendrick, Burton J. *The Life of Andrew Carnegie*. 2 vols. Garden City, N.Y.: Doubleday, 1932.

Hill, Frank P. *James Bertram: an Appreciation*. New York: Carnegie Corp., 1936.

Horrocks, Norman. *The Carnegie Corporation of New York and its Impact on Library Development in Australia: a Case-Study of Foundation Influence*. Unpublished Ph.D. Thesis, University of Pittsburgh, 1971.

Johnson, Alvin S. *Pioneer's Progress: an Autobiography*. New York: Viking, 1962.

_____ . *A Report to Carnegie Corporation of New York on the Policy of Donations to Free Public Libaries*. New York: Carnegie Corp., 1919.

Jordy, William H. *American Buildings and their Architects*. 4 vols. Garden City, N.Y.: Avalon Books, 1976.

Koch, Theodore Wesley. *A Book of Carnegie Libraries*. New York: Wilson, 1917.

Langmead, Stephen and Margaret Beckman. *New Library Design*. New York: Wiley, 1971.

Lester, Robert M. *Forty Years of Carnegie Giving: a Summary of the Benefactions of Andrew Carnegie and of the work of the Philanthropic Trusts which he Created*. New York: Scribner, 1941.

Miller, Durand R., comp. *Carnegie Grants for Library Buildings, 1890-1917*. New York: Carnegie Corp., 1943.

Munthe, William. *American Librarianship from a European Angle: an Attempt at an Evaluation of Policies and Activities*. Chicago: American Library Assocation, 1939.

Pevsner, Nikolaus. *A History of Building Types*. Princeton, N.J.: Princeton University Press, 1976.

Robertson, William. *Welfare in Trust: a History of the Carnegie United Kingdom Trust, 1913-1963*. Dunfermline: The Carnegie United Kingdom Trust, 1964.

Twombly, Robert C. *Frank Lloyd Wright: his Life and his Architecture*. New York: Wiley, 1979.

Wall, Joseph Frazier. *Andrew Carnegie*. New York: Oxford University Press, 1970.

Whiffen, Marcus. *American Architecture, 1607-1976*. Cambridge, Mass.: MIT Press, 1981.

Articles, pamphlets

Alexander, H.B. "The Sculpture and Inscription on the Los Angeles Public Library," *The Western Architect*, LXXXV (February, 1927) pp. 19-22.

Chapman, Alfred H. "Obituary." *The Journal of The Royal Architectural Institute of Canada*, XXVII, no. 2 (February, 1950).

Beckman, Margaret, John Black and Stephen Langmead. "In Search of Carnegie." *Ontario Library Review*, LXV (March, 1981) pp. 33-37 (Reprinted in *Expression*, Fall, 1981.)

Beckman, Margaret, John Black and Stephen Langmead. "Carnegie Libraries of Canada." *Canadian Library Journal*, XXXVIII, no. 6 (December, 1981), pp. 386-390.

"Boston Public Library." *The American Architect and Building News*, XX (April 6, 1895), p. 3.

Bow, Eric. "The Public Library Movement in Nineteenth Century Ontario." *Ontario Library Review*, LXVI (March, 1982), pp. 1-16.

Carnegie, Andrew. "The Library Gift Business." *Collier's*, LXXIII (June 5, 1909), pp. 14-15.

"Carnegie West Branch Library — Historic Landmark Renovation." *Lighting Design & Application*, X (November, 1980) pp. 26-30.

Cherry, Susan Spaeth. "Carnegies Live, but the Destiny of a Beloved Institution is unfolding in Mixed Triumph and Tragedy," *American Libraries*, XII (April, 1981), pp. 184-188, 218-222.

Langton, W.A. "Library Design." *The Canadian Architect and Builder* XV (1902), pp. 47-48.

Lowe, John Adams. "The Public Library Building Plan — II." *The Architectural Forum* (February, 1924), pp. 63-70.

"Mr. Carnegie's 'Investments'." *The Library Journal*, XXVII (June, 1902), p. 329.

Munn, Ralph. "Hindsight on the Gifts of Carnegie." *Library Journal*, LXXVI (December 1, 1951), pp. 1966-1970.

"Notes on the Erection of Library Bildings." *The Library Journal*, XL (April, 1915), pp. 243-247.

Olle, J.G.H. "Andrew Carnegie: the Unloved Benefactor." *Library World*, LXX (April, 1969), pp. 255-262.

Soule, Charles C. "Library Rooms and Buildings." Boston: Houghton, Mifflin (1902). American Library Association, Library Tract, no. 4, 24 p.

"The Philanthropy of Carnegie." *Ontario Library Review*, XIX (November, 1935), p. 142.

"Thanks, but no Thanks." *The Pittsburgh Press Roto* (July 17, 1983), pp. 9-12.

Other References

"Andrew Carnegie." Library Brochure from the Dunfermline Public Library, Scotland.

Bolek, Sandra J. "Carnegie Libraries in Ohio." Draft of a history of the Carnegie Libraries of Ohio, Cleveland, Ohio, 1982.

Bruce, Lorne. "Public Library Policies in Ontario, 1882-1920." Unpublished report, Guelph, Ontario, 1983.

"Carnegie Building" (formerly the Hamilton Public Library) 55 Main Street West. Unpublished report prepared for Hamilton LACAC (October, 1981).

Carnegie Corporation of New York. "List of Library Bildings in United States, Canada, United Kingdom and other English-speaking Countries. March, 1913." This date has been crossed out and December 31, 1915 written in hand. A letter signed Jas. Bertram indicates that the list is accurate if it is recognized as a list of promised grants. Many names in the list have been crossed out, with others written in.

Fraser and Browne, Architects, Thunder Bay, Ontario. "Restorations Proposed for the Brodie Street Resource Library." Third draft of a report on the Fort William Carnegie Library and the possibilities of renovation without destroying the original character of its design, 1979.

Lambert, Phyllis. "Notes on Libraries: development of form and use." Unpublished report, Montreal (January, 1981).

Neale, Christopher. "The First Carnegie Free Library." Unpublished essay. Dunfermline Scotland, 1976.

Illustration Credits

All photographs are by John Black unless otherwise identified below.

Sketches and architectural drawings are by Stephen Langmead.

Maps are by Marie Puddister, Cartographer, Department of Geography, University of Guelph.

The authors and publisher are grateful to the following photographers and organizations for the following pictures reproduced in this work:

Brantford Public Library **16**
Carnegie Corporation of New York **24**
Chatham Public Library **10**
Collingwood Public Library **28**
Cornwall Public Library (from files of Standard Freeholder) **37**
Horst Ehricht **65**, **66**, **68**, **76**
Fort Frances Public Library and Museum **142**, **150**
Guelph Public Library **35**
Hamilton Public Library **82**
Kenora Public Library **86**
Kitchener Public Library **53**, **139**
Stephen Langmead **135**
The Moon: Vol. II, no. 39, February 21, 1903 **41** , **59**
North Bay Public Library **162**
Orillia Public Library **44**
Ottawa Public Library **63**, **110**
Penetanguishene Public Library **86**
St. Catharines Public Library **125**
Sarnia Public Library and Art Gallery **109**, **138**, **156**
Sault Ste. Marie Public Library **35**
Thunder Bay Public Library **136**, **169**
Waterloo Public Library **90**, **102**, **139**
Windsor Public Library Board **31**, **138**
Stephen Wolowich of Fred Bird and Associates **70**, **71**, **73**, **74**, **79**, **98**, **99**, **121**, **133**
James Wilson, Fife, Scotland **172**
Woodstock Public Library and Art Gallery **27**

Index

Index of Places:
(Ontario – unless otherwise indicated)

Aberdeen, Scotland 18
Allegheny, Pennsylvania 17
Amherstburg 11, 12, **153**, 154, 157
Arthur 55
Aurora 21
Aylmer 107, 127, 140, 158
Ayr 42, 50, 120, 126, 140, 157
Ayr, Scotland 18

Barrie 79, 97, 107, 114, 126, 140, 141, 157, 167
Bangor, Maine 171
Beaverton 126, 140, 143-145, 157
Berlin   see Kitchener
Boston, Massachusetts 164
Bracebridge 45, 157, 163
Braddock, Pennsylvania 18
Brampton 91, 97, 158, 165
Brantford 21, 31, **55**, 76, **77**, **83**, 89, 107, **108**, 115, 120, **121**, 134, **136**, 137, 157, 173
Brockville 31, 89, 106, **108**, 120, 157, 175
Brussels 43, 104, 106, 157

Caledonia 55
Calexico, California 171
Cambridge (Galt) 47, **75**, 89, **111**, 126, 158, **169**, 175
Cambridge (Hespeler) 107, 115, 157, 175
Cambridge (Preston) 115, 126, 140, 158, **172**
Campbellford **71**, 93, 127, 140, 154, 157
Cedar Rapids, Iowa 170
Chatham **10**, 11, 31, 89, 107, 134, 137, 158, 163, 165
Cleveland, Ohio 26, 143, 170
Clinton 87, 94, **95**, 132, 157
Chicago, Illinois 134
Collingwood **28**, 30, 32, 33, 45, 89, 154, 158, 163, 165
Cornwall 11, 28, **37**, 38-39, 89, 137, 158, 165

Dresden 58, **59**, 157, 167
Dundas 21, 97, 106, 114, 140, 158
Dunfermline, Scotland 17, 18, 60
Durham **68**, 127, 140, 157

Edinburgh, Scotland 18
Elmira **67**, 120, 127, 140-141, 157, 167, **168**
Elora 88, 91, **142**, 143, 157
Essex 127, **150**, 157
Etobicoke 158, 177
Exeter 85, 115, 140, 157

Fairchild, Iowa 18
Fergus 47, 57, **89**, 91, 127, 140, 154, 157
Forest 42, 64, **75**, 105, 127, 140, 157
Fort Francis 11, 115, 140, **142**, **150**, 157
Fort William   see Thunder Bay (Fort William)
Fort Worth, Texas 173

Galt   see Cambridge (Galt)
Gananoque 55
Glencoe 50, 94, **95**, 132, 157
Goderich **80**, 89, 107, **109**, 132, 157, 165, 167, 175
Grand Valley **41**, 42, 43, 45, 47, 50, 58, 104, 115, 127, 140, 157
Gravenhurst 94, 115, 132, 157, 175
Grimsby 140, 141, 157
Guelph 11, 28, 33-34, **35**, 46, 81, 89, 106, 127, 134, 151, 152, 154, 158, 163, 164, 165

Hamilton 21, 23, 34, 43, **44**, 56, 81, **82**, 84, 88, 89, 117, **122**, 137, **140**, 158
Hanover 26, 29, 49, 58, **72**, 84, 107, 126, 127, **128**, 140, 157
Harriston 49, 58, 105, 107, 126, 127, **129**, 140, 157, 163
Hespeler   see Cambridge (Hespeler)
Homestead, Pennsylvania 46

Ingersoll 84, 85, **124**, 126, 157
Inverness 18

Jedburg, Scotland 18

Kemptville 11, 115, 132, 157
Kenora 11, 85, **86**, 157
Kincardine 46, 157
Kingston 21
Kingsville 115, 127, 157
Kitchener 31, 47, 51, 52, **53**, 57, 87, 89, 137, **139**, 151, 158, 163, 164, 165, 166

Leamington 158
Lindsay 29, 31, 45, 89, 107, **110**, 120, 134, 157, 165, 175
Listowel 57, 69, 126, 127, 140, **146**, 157
London **20**, 23, 56, 88
London, England 11
Lucknow 47, **48**, 49, 51, 97, 157, 167

Machell's Corners   see Aurora
Manchester, England 46
Markdale 50, **92**, 93, 115, 157
Merrickville 55
Merritton 94, 132, 140, 157
Midland 46, 158
Millbank 55
Milverton 50, 126, **131**, 140, 157, 167
Mimico   see Etobicoke
Mitchell **72**, 126, 134, 140, 143, **146**, 157, **168**
Mount Forest **123**, 127, **130**, 140, 157

Nairobi, Kenya 11
Newark   see Niagara-on-the-Lake
New Hamburg 115, 157
New Liskeard 11, 88, 126, 134, 137, **153**, 154, 157
New Orleans, Louisiana 64
New York, New York 30, 49, 52, 56
Niagara-on-the Lake 21
Niagara Falls 158, **162**, 166
North Bay 158, **162**

Norwich 50, 157
Norwood **74**, 93, 94, 132, 157

Orangeville 90, 91, 97, 157, 167
Orillia **44**, 45, 46, 88, 157, 167
Oshawa 88, 158
Ottawa 28, 34, 36, 60, 61, **63**, 89, **110**, 127, 134, 137, 158, 163, 164
Ottawa – West Branch 36, 157
Otterville 55
Owen Sound 29, 93, 157, 167

Paisley 55
Palmerston 47, **48**, 49, 127, 157
Paris 21, 31, 89, 157, 163
Parkhill 114, 140, 157
Parry Sound 29
Pembroke **73**, 132, 134, **135**, 145, 147, 148, 157
Penetanguishene 84, **86**, 154, 157, 167
Perth 106, 107, 158
Peterborough 126, 158
Peter Head, Scotland 18
Petrolia 55
Picton 64, **79**, 81, 91, 157, 163
Pittsburgh, Pennsylvania 18, 26, 30, 33, 60
Port Arthur   see Thunder Bay (Port Arthur)
Port Elgin 46, 120, 157
Port Hope 127, 140, 157
Preston   see Cambridge (Preston)

Renfrew 81, 93, 94, 157

St. Catharines 28, 39, 40, 47, 64, 89, **125**, 126, 137, 145, 158, 163
St. Marys 43, **78**, 87, 89, 115, **116**, 120, 154, 155, 157, 163
St. Thomas 40, 56, 89, 137, 158, 163, 164, 165, 170
Sarnia 11, 31, 89, 107, **109**, 134, 137, **138**, **156**, 158, 164, 165, 173
Sault Ste. Marie 28, **35**, 36, 49, 158
Seaforth 26, **69**, 87, 126, **133**, 145, 157, 167
Shelburne **77**, 105, 107, **122**, 143, **144**, 148, 157
Simcoe 57, 132, 158
Skibo Castle, Scotland 30, 60, 61, 81, 84
Smiths Falls 31, 34, 62, **63**, 64, **70**, **71**, 89, 107, 115, 127, **129**, 137, 143, 158, 165
Stirling 50, 115, 127, 140, 157
Stirling, Scotland 18
Stouffville 50, 85, 94, 115, 132, 158
Stratford 28, 31, 36, **37**, 47, 56, 89, 107, **111**, 126, 141, 157, 163, 164
Strathroy 55

Tavistock 50, 57, 84, 93, **131**, 157
Teeswater **50**, 51, 57, 126, 140, 157
Thessalon 55
Thorold 56, 85, 91, 104, 140, 157
Thunder Bay (Fort William) 115, 134, **136**, 137, 157, **169**, 170, 175
Thunder Bay (Port Arthur) 55
Tilbury 54, 55
Tillsonburg 57, 127, 140, 158
Toronto 23, 61, 62, 96, 100, 101, 105, 114, 117, 137, 140, 170, 177

Toronto – Central Reference Library 96, 97, **98**, 114, 132, 137, 158
  Annette Branch 97, **98**, 157, 170, 177
  Beaches Branch 100, 105, 117, **121**, 132, 157
  Dovercourt Branch 97
  Earlscourt Branch 115
  High Park Branch 100, 105, 117, 132, 157
  Queen & Lisgar Branch 97, 158
  Riverdale Branch **79**, 97, 106, 132, 157
  Wychwood Branch **74**, **99**, 100, 105, **106**, 115, 117, 120, 132, 157
  Western Branch   See Annette Branch
  Yorkville Branch 97, 132, **133**, 157, 170
Toronto Junction   see Toronto – Annette Branch

Walkerton 46, 127, 134, 140, 157
Wallaceburg 47, 64, 157, 167
Washington, D.C. 29
Waterloo 11, 47, 85, 87, 89, **90**, 93, **102**, 107, 115, 137, **139**, 158, 163, 164, 165, 167
Watertown, Wisconsin 170
Watford **67**, **78**, 120, 127, **130**, 140, 157
Welland 93, 94, 95, 141, 143, 157, 175
West Toronto   see Toronto – Annette Branch
Weston   see York (Borough)
Whitby 140, 158
Wick, Scotland 18
Windsor 11, 28, 29, 30, **31**, 32, 56, 89, 137, **138**, 149, 151, 158, 163
Woodstock 12, **65**, **66**, 120, **122**, 134, 137, 157, **178**

York   see Toronto
York (Borough) **73**, 126, 157, 177

Nominal Index:

Adams, Dr. W.G.S. 176
Adamson, J.H. 143
Aitchison, James 141
American Federation of Labor 46
American Library Association 166, 170
Anderson, Edwin H. 26, 33, 39
Anderson, Col. James 17
Armstrong, Mrs. H. 93

Badgley, Sidney R. 39, 145
Bain, James 52, 96, 100
Baird, Miss Jean 93
Barnett, J. Davis 38
Bartlet, N.A. 32
Baxter, James 43, 87
Bayley, G.M. 127, 143